For Sonny Dixon

Lucy B. Long

The Henry Ford Era

at
Richmond Hill,
Georgia

by

Franklin Leslie Long, Ph.D.
&
Lucy Bunce Long

The Henry Ford Era at Richmond Hill, Georgia

Design and printing by
Darien Printing & Graphics
101 Broad Street, Darien, GA 31305 • (912)437-4251

Books available for purchase from
Dr. and Mrs. F. Leslie Long
186 Lincoln Circle
Richmond Hill, GA 31324

Library of Congress Catalog Card Number: 98-74051

ISBN 0-9667610-0-6

ACKNOWLEDGEMENTS

EVER SINCE MR. AND MRS. HENRY FORD PASSED AWAY in 1947 and 1950, respectively, we have had a very strong feeling that someone should record for future generations what the Fords had done for the Richmond Hill area over a period of nearly twenty-five years. However, after the Fords had passed away and the plantation was sold, we were very busy with our careers and moved from the area. We didn't seem to find the time to record what we knew about it. Neither of us had training in historical writing and we kept thinking someone else would write about it.

We retired in 1982 and returned to Richmond Hill. We always knew we wanted to retire at Richmond Hill since it had made such a strong impression on us during the Ford years. No one had yet written the valuable and interesting history of the Fords here. By that time many of those who had witnessed what the Fords did in the coastal area of Georgia had passed away.

In 1987 we helped organize the Richmond Hill Historical Society. Since that time it has become even more evident that this Ford history should be preserved. We finally decided that it was our responsibility, to the memory of Mr. and Mrs. Ford, to record what we could and publish this history before it was lost. We began getting our photographs together and started working on it.

We have numerous people to thank for their cooperation, assistance, and continuous encouragement during this process. We are most grateful to Mr. Ford Bryan, a Ford Archives volunteer researcher, for his assistance, encouragement, and advice during the preparation of this book. He first urged us to write it when we visited the archives in 1985. He, having published several books about the Fords, had helpful suggestions.

In addition to Mr. Bryan, we wish to thank Dr. Charles Hanson, Head of Access Services of the Ford Archives, for his ready cooperation and for granting us permission to reproduce and use some of their Richmond Hill photographs in this book. Also, we would like to thank Ms. Linda Skolarus and Ms. Cathy Lee Tendresse of the Research Library for their great help and patience in locating Richmond Hill Plantation material for us. Ms. Mia C. Temple, of the photographic reproduction services was very patient and helpful to us. We appreciate and thank Dr. Donn Werling and Dr. David Lewis, both of the University of Michigan, for their encouragement when they visited Richmond Hill. Several members of the Henry Ford Heritage Association have been very helpful. Dick Folsom not only encouraged us but supplied some of the photographs from Mrs. Rufus Wilson's collection.

In addition to the numerous photos we had collected over a sixty year period, we obtained numerous photos from local residents, or from those who had been here during the Ford days. We would especially like to thank Miss Kay Speir for loaning us numerous negatives of key subjects and operations on the plantation. These photos made possible the showing of many aspects of the plantation operations that otherwise would not have been possible. Buck and Bertie Rahn were very helpful in sharing their knowledge and photographs with us. Thanks go to the Martin family for the photograph of Mary Lou. Mrs. Lora Hanson, Mrs. Ray Newman's niece, furnished a photograph of Mr. Ray Newman, a former superintendent of the Ford Plantation. John Mahaffey provided a photo of Mr. Bascom Mahaffey who was in charge of the garage operations. Mrs. Janie Lanier Mainord furnished a photograph of students dancing in the ballroom of the Community House. Thanks to Charles Boles for helping in some identifications and for a photograph of Mr. Ford and George Washington Carver. Mrs. Joanne Sasser gave us a photo of the entrance gate to the Ford residence. Thanks to Jackie Mitchum for helping identify members of the Glee Club.

Our grateful appreciation also to Mr. Charles M. Williamson, III, "Charlie," and Mrs. Elise F. Hannah of Darien Printing and Graphics, for their helpful suggestions and patience.

Last, but certainly not least, we are deeply grateful to Buddy Sullivan for reading the manuscript, making helpful suggestions, and for his continuous encouragement.

Despite our best efforts, no doubt, there are those that we failed to mention. To all those unnamed individuals who have been helpful in numerous ways please accept our sincere thanks.

Franklin Leslie Long & Lucy Bunce Long

CONTENTS

INTRODUCTION

RICHMOND HILL IS A SMALL TOWN IN COASTAL SOUTHEAST GEORGIA about twenty miles south of Savannah, in Bryan County on U.S. Highway 17 about two miles east of Interstate Highway 95. In recent years it has become a "bedroom" of Savannah. Not so in 1925 when Mr. and Mrs. Henry Ford became interested in it. At that time its name was Ways Station and it had only two gas stations, two general stores, and about six houses in what is now the city limits. Highway 17 was a narrow paved road but there was no other paved road in the vicinity. There were many miles of dirt, and often muddy, roads extending about fifteen miles east to the coast.

In giving lectures in the area, a question often asked is why did Mr. and Mrs. Ford become interested in a little place like Richmond Hill (then Ways Station). The answer lies, in part, in their association with some of their friends. There were four men who were good friends and who often traveled together. They were: Henry Ford, Harvey Firestone, Thomas A. Edison, and John Burroughs. Edison had a research laboratory in Ft. Myers, Florida. The Fords had a home across the street from the laboratory and would visit once or twice a year. In travelling to Ft. Myers, Burroughs would often accompany them . Whether travelling by boat or train they would pass through the Richmond Hill (Ways Station) area. Burroughs was a naturalist and knew a great deal about the flora and fauna of the area. He reportedly told the Fords that in all his travels he knew of no other area that had more natural beauty than the Richmond Hill area and he thought they should buy land in the area and build themselves a winter home here. After investigating more thoroughly they decided to do just that. Mrs. Ford said they had no privacy in Ft. Myers anymore and were bothered by "gate crashers." It was apparent from the start that the Fords were not only interested in just a home here but to expand on their humanitarian projects as they had elsewhere.

In 1925 Mr. Ford started buying land in the Richmond Hill area. In the beginning, the land was purchased through Cooper Realty Company in Savannah. By 1935 he had accumulated about 70,000 acres or more than 100 square miles. One might wonder how he was able to accumulate that much land. Remember, that was during the height of the depression when there were very few jobs available and even those paid very little. Even those who had property had the expense of keeping it up and paying taxes on it. Therefore, when offered what seemed to be a good price, they were willing to sell. However, not all property was sold to Mr. Ford. A few of the relatively smaller landowners did not sell. The Miner family who owned about ninety acres at the intersection of US Highway 17 and State Highway 144, then called "The Crossroads," did not sell. Two Miner brothers ran businesses there, one a gas station and the other a gas/grocery store. Another parcel that did not sell was at the community of Keller, about ten miles east of Richmond Hill. It was owned by the Carpenters. Gordon Carpenter ran a country store there and continued to run it until he passed away in 1957. Another parcel east of Keller owned by the Hardens did not sell. However, some of the Hardens worked for the plantation. Other homesites, east of Keller, that did not sell was property of the Smiths and Jones. Their descendants still live on the property.

The large plantations were the first to be sold to Mr. Ford, such as Cherry Hill, Richmond,

Strathy Hall, Whitehall, Cottenham, and Kilkenny. Some of these involved thousands of acres. These plantations generally were not owned by local residents but by relatively wealthy people who lived elsewhere and the plantations were a "getaway" for them and sometimes used as hunting lodges. There was a lot of game in the area to hunt, especially deer. Since these large tracts of land were more or less a luxury to the owners, they were soon sold to Mr. Ford. The acquisition of some of the smaller parcels was more time consuming due, in part, to the difficulty of obtaining a clear title. Some of the parcels were handed down from generation to generation and titles were not clear. Eventually, Mr. Ford owned seventy-five or eighty thousand acres or more than 110 square miles. The total was even more if some of the marsh land of questionable ownership is included. In all there were at least five hundred different parcels of land bought. Considering all, Mr. Ford probably wound up owning ninety-nine percent of the land in Bryan County lying east of US Highway 17 to the coast.

Much of the land in coastal Bryan County, including the land Mr. Ford had purchased, was low-land. Some of it had standing water on it most of the year. Some other portions had standing water on it part of the year. These conditions were conducive to the breeding of mosquitoes which carried malaria fever. Mr. Ford, of course, recognized these problems and immediately began a large drainage project to eliminate standing water and to drain low areas to reduce the incidence of malaria fever. This project was very extensive and included draining a large portion of the 75,000 acres. To begin with topographic surveys were made and the drainage ditches laid out. Much machinery was required to dig the canals and large ditches, particularly through the swampy areas. Bulldozers and tremendous amounts of manual labor were used to clear the right-of-way and large draglines dug the canals and ditches. The smaller secondary ditches were dug with smaller machinery. Even smaller ditches were dug using manual labor. Road building machinery was used to construct roads to previously inaccessible areas.

While the drainage project was underway the clinic was built. A survey had shown that almost one hundred percent of the population suffered from malaria fever. In February 1937, malaria control work was begun by Mr. Ford. Advisors from the Georgia State Board of Health and a representative from Winthrop Chemical Company which manufactured atabrine helped plan the program. Twenty-one nurses were employed for one week. Then eighteen were used for about three weeks longer. After that, Mrs. Clark and Nurse Reed could take care of the work. Areas were blocked off to be visited by a nurse. The nurse visited each house first thing in the morning and gave the tablet of atabrine. She went back after lunch and gave a second tablet and left a tablet to be taken at night. The people took the medicine or the employee lost his job and housing so there wasn't any trouble in getting them to take the medicine. Children were given only quinine. In February another blood smear was made. Only two who had the treatment were still positive. During the malaria survey a hookworm survey was also done and the positive ones received hookworm treatment later. The nurses were provided with transportation to go out to the patients' homes to give the malaria treatment. Often times the dirt roads were muddy and sometimes the vehicle would get stuck. The nurses persisted and, if necessary, would walk to get to their patients. A medical doctor from Savannah, Dr. C. F. Holton, was employed to come to the clinic once a week to treat the more stubborn cases or, if needed, to come more often. If Dr. Holton could not come, Dr. John Sharpley would come. Mrs. Constance Clark was head of the clinic and coordinated all the work. She was assisted by Mrs.

Sam Reed, affectionally known as "Nurse Reed." She was a very good and faithful nurse with unbelievable patience.

In 1936 Mr. and Mrs. Ford built their home on the banks of the Great Ogeechee River. Without doubt, a considerable amount of time was spent by the Fords in planning their home. At the time of their planning, an old plantation home in Savannah, "The Hermitage" came up for sale. It was the property of the Port Authority of Savannah who had acquired the property for industrial purposes. Prior to the Civil War, the Hermitage Plantation, among other things, was in the business of making brick. They made brick that later became known as "Savannah Gray Brick." Prior to the ownership of the Hermitage by the Ports Authority of Savannah the property was owned by the Judge McAlpin family. They did not live in "The Hermitage" and it had been unoccupied for years and had badly deteriorated. However, it was veneered with "Savannah Gray Brick," a much sought-after brick for home construction in the area. The Fords looked at it, liked what they saw, and bought it. They were primarily interested in the brick it contained. No more "Savannah Gray Brick" were being made. The supply was short and the demand was great. They had it torn down brick by brick and brought to Richmond Hill. There each brick was thoroughly cleaned by hand and the bricks used to build their home. The site they chose for their home was where once stood a rice plantation home called "Richmond." We consider the site to the be the most beautiful of all building sites on the Great Ogeechee River. The Fords named their home "Richmond."

When Mr. Ford bought the property, the ruins of an old rice mill which had operated on the rice plantation prior to the Civil War was on the property not too distant from the residence. In the debris was found the old steam engine which had powered the rice mill. Mr. Ford had it placed on a railroad car and shipped to Dearborn, Michigan where it was restored and put in like-new condition. The old rice mill building was completely restored and the rice mill engine was used to pull a generator which furnished electricity for the Ford residence. This was the quietest running steam engine I have ever seen. It was simply unbelievable that an engine of that size and that old could run so smoothly and quietly. I have stood beside it many times and listened in amazement. Standing within a foot of the flywheel, I could feel the air movement created by the flywheel, but heard no sound other than a slight hissing sound of the steam passing through the engine. I have the idea that the mechanic, or mechanics, who restored the engine knew that Mr. Ford would be listening to it and that prompted a superior job. Two wood fired steam boilers furnished steam to run the engine and to furnish heat. As I recall only one boiler was used at the time. The building was first called the rice mill but soon became to be called the powerhouse. An underground tunnel was constructed between the powerhouse and the residence, an estimated distance of 1100 feet. The tunnel was approximately six feet high and six feet wide. Through the tunnel ran the electricity, water, and heat to the residence. The Ford residence was not equipped with air conditioning since they were here during winter and early Spring. Mr. Ford would occasionally walk through the tunnel from the residence to the powerhouse and vice versa. In the upstairs of the powerhouse Mr. Ford had a jeweler's desk. I was told by the caretaker that he occasionally worked on watches there. He also had part of the chassis of an old Model T up there. I doubt that he ever worked with it. It probably was just a reminder of days gone by.

Another interesting part of the old rice mill was the tall brick chimney that had survived since the Civil War. Only the very top had been damaged by lighting. There was an underground tunnel from the old steam boilers in the rice mill out to the tall chimney about 75 feet away. The ingenuity here was incredible. They needed a strong updraft to carry the smoke away and create enough draft to make the wood fire burn well. Large metal smokestacks were not readily available in those days. They would build a fire in the base of the tall chimney, and after it had been going for a while the heat going up the chimney would create a suction back through the tunnel to the boilers. The boilers would then be fired and the chimney would create enough draft to make the wood burn faster and give more heat per unit of time thus giving more steam to operate the steam engine. I guess no one knows who figured this out but it certainly was very clever.

In 1937 Mr. and Mrs. Ford built the Martha-Mary Chapel at Richmond Hill. They named it in honor of their mothers. Her mother was named Martha and his mother was named Mary. This is not the only chapel they built. There were five others, four in Michigan and one in Massachusetts. The one in Richmond Hill is the largest having side rooms at the rear on each side of the building providing extra space for participants. Two white columns flank the entrance and it has a balcony. The construction is wood, all of which was produced here on the plantation and, of course, nothing but the best was used. The floors are all beautifully varnished heart of pine. The chapel was located near the school and each school morning the entire student body attended a thirty minute devotional service in the chapel. It was non-denominational and usually consisted of singing religious songs, and included a choir, reading of scripture, reading or reciting of an appropriate poem, and prayer. A very fine organ was provided by Mr. and Mrs. Ford. Part of the time Sunday School services were also held, all by members of the community. The participants and congregation included those other than Ford employees and family. Programs for the Sunday service were printed in the Ford Industrial Arts and Trade School. Printing was taught by Miss Mary Rogers and she was responsible for seeing that the programs were printed correctly and on time. The chapel was also used for special services such as weddings. In fact, the authors, were married there June 20, 1943.

The most impressive building on the plantation, except for the Ford residence, was the Community House. It was a very large building with nineteen bedrooms, eighteen bathrooms, lounges for ladies and gentlemen, a spacious kitchen, a formal living room, a large dining room capable of seating approximately sixty, and a very large ballroom for dancing. Words are grossly inadequate to express the many wonderful and great things that were enjoyed in this building, both educational and social. I called it the "Cultural Center of Richmond Hill" and truly it was. It was located adjacent to the chapel and near the school. One of the very important things it was used for was for the teaching of home economics and not just the basics but to the fullest extent of all the social graces. Dancing was taught in the huge ballroom. It was also used for school social functions such as banquets and school parties. It was used by the community for social affairs and dancing. A hostess lived in the building and was on duty at all times.

In teaching home economics, the classes lived at the Community House for a week at the time on a rotational basis. Thus the students lived and learned home economics there. The teacher taught them everything imaginable, even the proper way to make up a bed. They were taught how to plan a meal, how to shop for the ingredients, how to prepare food, the proper way to cook the food, the correct way to set the table, and how to serve the food correctly. All possible needs of silver and china were furnished to serve the meal in courses. I have often said that Emily Post would have been proud of them. Even today, more than fifty years later, the training these girls received shows through in their superior standards of etiquette and behavior, including in their homes.

Mr. and Mrs. Ford liked folk dancing and they hired a lady from Savannah, Mrs. Ebba Thomson, to come out to the Community House and teach dancing to the students one day a week. When the Fords were here the students had dancing classes every school day. Sometimes Mr. Ford's orchestra would come down when the Fords were here and play for the dances. In the absence of the orchestra, phonograph records produced by the orchestra, were available to play for the dances. In the early stages of teaching the dances, the piano was used. The pianist was paid by Mr. Ford. They were mostly quadrille type dances with the calls on the record. Also, there were some records for teaching ballroom type dances for couples. These were mostly waltzes which Mr. and Mrs. Ford liked. Along with the dances, students were taught ballroom manners. One did not walk across the dance floor but around it. One did not chew gum and, of course, no food. If a boy wanted to ask a girl to dance with him, he must walk around the outside of the dance floor and when he came to her he must bow and ask her to dance with him. If she chose to dance with him she must rise and curtsy and then they may dance. After they had finished dancing he must walk back with her to her seat and after she was seated he may walk away. Compare that to the "manners" of today. The teacher and students would occasionally put on a demonstration of their learned accomplishments in a dance program. Parents and other interested persons would be invited. It was very interesting to see not only their accomplishments in dancing but the ballroom manners they had learned and practiced. No other school in the area taught dancing or had any such nice facilities. I doubt there were any other such facilities in the state. Schools from the surrounding area would bring groups of students to the Community House to observe the dancing.

The adults of the community were impressed by the student dancing and liked it so much they soon formed an adult dancing club. They met twice a month at the Community House, learned the dances, and enjoyed them very much. A committee would be appointed to serve refreshments in the dining room after the dances.

Mr. Ford did so much for the community and school that it almost seems unbelievable. He added four rooms onto the Richmond Hill School Building including a chemistry and physics laboratory. State school officials considered it to be the best equipped high school laboratory in the state. He installed visual education equipment in the school. This included a movie projector, projection room and films. Some movies were shown at night. I usually ran the projector for the school when they had night movies. Also installed was a complete intercom system between the principal's office and all classrooms. This was in the late 1930's about sixty years ago, when other schools did not have such advanced educational facilities.

Mr. Ford built, furnished, and operated a lunchroom for the students and teachers. This lunchroom was completed in the late thirties and was probably the first lunch served to students and teachers in Georgia. Some schools had installed what was called a "soup kitchen" but, of course, did not serve a complete meal. Thanks to Mr. and Mrs. Ford, these lunches were served free of charge to all students and teachers. The students were taught exceptionally good table manners including the proper use of eating utensils. The students lined up outside the door until they were told they may come in. The boys were taught to pull out the chairs for the girls to sit before they could sit down. In a rare case where the boy did not do that he was sent to the principal's office for punishment.

Next time he chose to pull out the chair. Whatever the punishment was, it obviously worked since there was no more problem with that again.

There were lots of fruits and vegetables grown on the plantation here. The lady in charge of the lunchroom, Mrs. Pearl Carpenter, together with her help, canned large amounts of fruits and vegetables during the summer in June, July, and August, to be served in the lunchroom during the school year. Some of the students were hired to help with this project. All the equipment for processing these large amounts was provided by Mr. Ford.

Mr. Ford supplemented the teachers salaries. This was extremely important in the advancement of the school program at Richmond Hill. At that time, the late thirties and early forties, state pay for teachers was only seventy-five dollars per month for nine months. Mr.Ford supplemented at least thirty dollars per month. This meant that teachers in the Richmond Hill School received one hundred and five dollars per month instead of seventy-five. Also, the teachers were paid for twelve months because Mr. Ford gave them a summer job and paid them the same as if they were teaching. Consequently, there were numerous applicants for teaching positions at Richmond Hill. Thus, the Board of Education and Trustees were able to choose from a large base and hire only the very best qualified teachers. This resulted in a staff of superior teachers at Richmond Hill. With excellent facilities and teachers, the Richmond Hill School system was outstanding and was recognized as such in the state of Georgia. There were many other factors that contributed to the desire to teach at Richmond Hill. Among them was the fact that Mr. Ford built and operated a teacherage within a block of the school for the teachers. The teachers could live there at a very reasonable cost and only a short block from the school. Some teachers did not have an automobile and this was very beneficial to them. He also built a home for the principal adjacent to the school. Today Richmond Hill has excellent schools and part of it is due to the outstanding start they got in the early thirties, thanks to Mr. Ford.

Mr. Ford built and operated an Industrial Arts and Trade School for Richmond Hill students. There the students were taught numerous trades such as machine shop, welding, mechanical drawing and carpentry. Ford paid all costs including instructors, equipment, supplies and utilities. There were no costs whatsoever to students. There were also free night classes for adults. Students could work in the Trade School during the summer if they chose to and were paid for their work. Students could also work for an hour or two after school and on Saturday mornings, thus earning a little spending money.

At that time there were separate schools for blacks. Small one-room schoolhouses were located in the various communities. Mr. Ford built and operated the George Washington Carver School for the blacks. He had a survey made to determine the highest educational level of the blacks. It turned out to be the fifth grade. Mr. Ford started out with six grades and added a grade each year as they advanced. This seemed to be a very unique and common sense approach to educating the blacks. Mr. Ford built a teacherage for the Carver teachers. He also built and operated a lunchroom for students and teachers. In addition, he built and operated an Industrial Arts Shop for the students. This school was very beneficial to the blacks. Many who went through that school will today attest to the fact that Carver School did more for them than any other thing that Mr. Ford did and it got them started toward a better life. Adjacent to the school, Mr. Ford prepared a field where the students were taught how to grow and harvest crops.

Mr. Ford had a huge farming operation on the Plantation. The total amount of cultivated land probably exceeded three thousand acres. An indication as to the size of the farming operation can be gauged by the fact that in 1945 the plantation had forty-five tractors. One of the largest projects was the reclamation of some of the old rice fields. These fields had been abandoned since the Civil War and had grown up in trees and brush. The dams had long since been broken and the fields were periodically flooded by the tide. First, the dams were repaired to keep out the water. The fields were then cleared of trees and brush and the old canals and ditches restored. There were two of the old rice fields that were reclaimed. They were the Cherry Hill marsh and the Richmond marsh. The Cherry Hill marsh had three hundred acres and the Richmond marsh had two hundred acres.

For those not familiar with the old rice fields and how they were operated prior to the Civil War, a few words of explanation appear to be in order. The operation was a long, tedious, and sometimes complicated management of water, soil. and crop. The large rice fields were located in the marshes or swamps adjacent to the river. They were strategically located. They could not be so far toward the ocean that the water was too salty to grow rice and could not be located so far up the river that there was not sufficient tidal fluctuation to flood and drain the field at certain stages of growth. This area is usually referred to as the brackish water area. In growing rice, large dikes were built along the river and a flood gate installed so that water could be let in at high tide and let out at low tide. The flood gate had to be large in order to let in enough water during the time the tide was high. A large canal inside the dike transferred the main water supply around the field. The fields were divided into relatively small areas and these smaller areas received water through secondary ditches from the large canals. A series of small flood gates controlled the water to these smaller areas. Water was not only used to grow rice but was used to control weeds and grass. Rice was very tolerant to fresh or brackish water. The rice was planted and harvested by hand. It was a thriving industry prior to the Civil War and supplied a staple food for millions of people around the world. One rice planter in this area along the Great Ogeechee River produced a million pounds of rice in one year. The Cherry Hill marsh field was considered the better of the two marsh fields that were reclaimed. It had a higher percentage of organic matter and the soil physical condition was much better.

Mr. Harry G. Ukkelberg was in charge of the farming operations in addition to being director of the research laboratory. This was a logical arrangement since much of the research had to do with agriculture and a great deal of research was required to bring the old rice fields into production for modern day crops of that time. The old rice fields were divided into sections and areas within sections. After physical reclamation was complete, experimental plantings were made of oats and other indicator crops to assess the productivity and nutrient status problems. It was found that the soil would not adequately produce most vegetable crops. The question facing us was: "Why will it not produce these vegetable crops?" It thus became the responsibility of the research laboratory to identify the cause and determine the means of solving the problem. I can assure you it was not easy. In 1938 we set up soil testing equipment in the research laboratory. At that time information on soil testing was very limited. Only a few land grant universities were involved to any appreciable extent in soil testing. We began by sampling the soil in each area of each field. Using what information we could gather, we started testing the soil for various components. We sampled for acidity, nitrogen, phosphorus, potassium, calcium, magnesium, sulfur, boron, zinc, copper, manganese, molybdenum, and iron all of which are essential for plant growth. One of the first things we found was that the soil was much too acid to grow modern day vegetables. Rice of those early days was a very acid tolerant plant and grew well on acid soil. We also found that the plants were not getting enough phosphorus, not due to it not being there but mostly due to the undesirable form in which the phosphorus was present in the soil due to the high acidity. We also found that there was a slight deficiency of copper. A small application of copper sulfate corrected that. There were some other problems but these were the main ones.

Mr. Ford was extremely interested in this work. He always wanted to know how it was coming along. It is being partially explained here so the reader will get some idea as to how we went about accomplishing what Mr. Ford wanted us to do. Mr. Ford, of course, was paying all expenses and it was up to us to get the job accomplished. There was absolutely no problem in getting all the equipment and supplies we needed. We started out by working on the acidity problem. Each area of each section had been tested for acidity and recorded. These tests had been conducted in great detail. The results were recorded on detailed maps so that the soil could be treated according to its need. They differed to a considerable extent and had to be treated accordingly. To correct the soil acidity, we added finely ground dolomitic limestone, about ninety percent of which would pass a 100-mesh sieve. The finely ground material was used because it would react quicker and, therefore, correct the acidity sooner. This limestone is a mixture of about 60 percent calcium carbonate and about 40 percent magnesium carbonate. In addition to correcting the acidity, this limestone supplies calcium and magnesium, both of which are essential for plant growth. After each application of limestone had had time to react with the soil, another measure of acidity was made and, if needed, more limestone was applied. Some areas required as much as twenty tons of limestone per acre to reduce the soil acidity to a desirable range for growing vegetables.

Generous amounts of phosphorus were also applied. Decreasing the soil acidity with limestone also increased the availability of the phosphorus to the plants and thus helped to solve the phosphorus problem. Copper is essential for plant growth but very minute amounts are required . Thus, very small amounts of copper sulfate were applied to the soil to correct any possible copper deficiency. Although Mr. Ford fully supported the work and was extremely interested in it, I'm sure he was not aware of the complexity of the problem and the technicalities involved. But that was understandable. He didn't need to know. He expected us to solve the problem and we did. Mr. Harry Ukkelberg was in charge of this reclamation project and supervised it to completion. He deserves a great deal of credit for his hard work, persistence, and patience.

After the reclamation was complete, Mr. Ukkelberg started planting various vegetables and essentially all of them grew well and made good yields on these reclaimed rice fields. One of the best crops was Iceberg lettuce and eventually became the main crop grown in these fields. A lettuce packing shed was built and the packaged lettuce was marketed through a wholesale produce dealer in Savannah and shipped up and down the east coast. The amount of lettuce grown averaged about 140 acres per year. A profit was shown nine of the ten years it was grown which was, of course, a very good record and reflected good management, good weather, and hard work. Lettuce was grown until Mr. Ford passed away. Sweet corn and other crops were grown on these fields but not to the extent of lettuce. Other crops such as Irish potatoes, sweet potatoes, and soybeans were grown on the upland soils.

A point of interest to the reader may be how we marketed the sweet potatoes. When sweet potatoes are harvested the market is usually flooded and the price often drops very low – sometimes below the cost of production. To avoid this problem, a sweet potato treatment and storage house was built. In harvesting sweet potatoes, they are raw on each end where they are broken from the remainder of the root. Sometimes they will rot on these ends. Under ideal conditions, cork cells cover the raw ends and allows the potato to keep for a longer period of time. The ideal conditions for cork cell formation are 89 degrees Fahrenheit and 95 percent relative humidity. When the potatoes were harvested they were marketed until the price became too low and then they were placed in the treatment/storage house. The ideal conditions, as mentioned above, were created in this treatment/storage house and held that way for two weeks. This allowed cork cell formation on the ends of the potatoes and enabled them to keep for a longer period of time. They could then be sold at a more reasonable price. The potato house was large enough to hold 2500 bushels. All these things clearly document Mr. Ford's interest in agriculture and in a more reasonable price for farm produce.

Another interesting note about sweet potatoes may be of interest to the reader. The sweet potato variety that we normally planted was Puerto Rico. It is a good potato and the skin is red. Another very good potato came out that had a light colored skin. Mr. Ukkelberg decided to try them. They did not sell well at all. Apparently customers thought that a good sweet potato had to have a red skin and they didn't buy them. We had about 2000 bushels of these. We bought a barrel of red wax and using a large container and the wax, we coated the entire 2000 bushels. Thus, we had red skin potatoes. They sold like "hotcakes," and we could have sold a lot more had we had them. They were very good sweet potatoes.

Mr. Ford built and operated a huge sawmill. This operation was very beneficial to and extremely complementary to other operations he had going on the plantation. For example, some of the lumber was used in the many building construction projects on the plantation. The lumber was used in the construction of the community house, chapel, commissary, bakery, addition to Richmond Hill School, Industrial Arts and Trade School, school lunchroom, garage, houses for employees, fences, and various other construction jobs.

There is an interesting note about the amount of lumber produced at the sawmill. Mr. Ford had hired a full time forester for the plantation and he asked him to make a survey to determine how much timber was growing on the plantation each day. It turned out to be about 15,000 board feet per day. So Mr. Ford would not let them cut but that much per day. He said, in that way, the sawmill could operate indefinitely. However, when WWII came along and there was a great demand for lumber for the war effort, he let them saw to capacity which was 75-100 thousand board feet per day.

In 1936 Mr. Ford built a research laboratory at Richmond Hill to conduct research on the conversion of farm products into products usable in the automotive industry. He said that farmers were some of his best customers; they bought his cars, trucks, and tractors. He said he would like to return the favor by buying their products and using them in his automotive industry. He envisioned converting some of the farm products into plastics that could be used for automobile parts. Mr. Harry G. Ukkelberg was director of the laboratory. He had a degree in agriculture from the University of Minnesota and had worked on goldenrod as a source of rubber at the Thomas A. Edison Laboratory at Ft. Myers, Florida. He had been put in charge of that work after Mr. Edison had passed away. Mr. Ford hired him to be in charge of the research laboratory at Richmond Hill. Mr. Ford had become acquainted with him on visits to Ft. Myers. In February of 1938 I was hired by Mr. Ukkelberg to work in the research laboratory. I was just out of high school the previous year and was working on our family farm and, of course, did not have a college degree at that time but it gave me a chance to learn. My wife had a degree and taught mathematics and science in high school. During the summers she either worked in the laboratory or in the plantation office. As previously stated I worked in the laboratory on the soil testing program. I also worked on plant variety testing and plant analysis.

At one time Mr. Ford manufactured tires and he was interested in making rayon from local timber for possible use as tire cord. Mr. Ford hired two men from Savannah to work on this project. They were Frank McCall and Jack Oliver. Mr. McCall had worked for the Herty Foundation Laboratory in Savannah, a research laboratory devoted to research on paper making and rayon. Both of these men had degrees in chemistry. These two men were well qualified and devoted their full time to rayon and plastic research and what interesting research it was. Plastics research was in its infancy. Mr. Ukkelberg, was also in charge of the farming operations. So the laboratory became primarily an agricultural laboratory and a rayon and plastics laboratory.

The work accomplished in the laboratory was outstanding. Even though plastics was just getting started, this laboratory was successful in experimentally producing a lignin plastic from corn cobs that was suitable for gear shift knobs, distributor caps, as well as other parts. Similar plastics were made from sawdust. One of the interesting aspects of the plastics research was the result of combining ramie fiber with some of the plastics. Mr. Ukkelberg was growing ramie as one of the experimental crops. Ramie fiber is extremely strong. It has been reported to have more tensile strength than steel. When ramie fibers were molded into the plastic it made the plastic much stronger. The stronger the plastic the greater the possibility of using it for automotive parts.

Research on plastics from soybeans was conducted in Dearborn, rather than the Richmond Hill Research Laboratory. However, some of the field and laboratory research was conducted in Richmond Hill. Mr. Ford was also interested in soybeans for food and for oil for possible use in paint. Here at Richmond Hill at one time we were experimenting with 365 different varieties, strains, or selections of soybeans. The experimental field plantings consisted of three fifty foot rows of each plus more detailed field experiments with the most promising varieties. Yield of each in the field was determined and the oil content of each in the laboratory. Additional criteria were used in evaluating each variety such as height, maturity date, shatter resistance, and seed size. All of these criteria are important in determining the best variety.

Rayon was made in the laboratory from sweet gum and black gum trees grown on the plantation. Rayon had been made from pine but not from gum trees. Mr. Ford had the forester make a survey and found out that there was more sweet gum and black gum on the plantation than there was pine. Therefore, Mr. Ford was particularly interested in making a product from them since they did not have a large use like pine. Mr. McCall and Mr. Oliver continued to work on rayon and plastics and rayon was successfully made from black gum and sweet gum trees. Although not made into tire cord, it was shown that it could be made from these trees. Some of the rayon made in the laboratory was used to make Mr. Ford a pair of socks. Mr. Ford wore these socks around the plantation. I doubt that anyone has ever seen a prouder man than Mr. Ford when he wore these socks around the plantation. He would show them off by pulling up his pants leg and pointing to his socks and say, "See that – that used to be a black gum tree."

These are just some examples of the things that were accomplished in the research laboratory and hopefully will serve to show Mr. Ford's broad, varied, and intense interest in agriculture. Unfortunately, a fire destroyed the laboratory before it could reach its full potential and was not rebuilt.

One of the nicest things Mr. Ford did for the employees was to build them houses. He built about 235 of these houses. To begin with he did not charge any rent. They were furnished free of charge. However, later the Internal Revenue Service forced him to make a charge. He then started charging $15 per month. He immediately raised employee pay by $15 per month. The houses were appreciated and enjoyed by employees. They were kept in excellent condition, both from the standpoint of Mr. Ford and the employee. If I may do so, I would like to relate a personal experience concerning the housing. When my wife and I had planned to get married, I went to the superintendent of the plantation, who was then Mr. Jack Gregory, and told him I was going to get married and would like to rent one of the houses that had been built. His reply was: "No, go pick you out a lot and draw you up some plans and I will build you one." He did just that and I will never forget it as long as I live. We lived in that house until after Mr. and Mrs. Ford died and the place was sold. I will always feel a deep debt of gratitude to Mr. and Mrs. Ford. Still today, some people ask me what kind of car I drive. Could I drive anything but a Ford product? The answer is "no." Mr. and Mrs. Ford are gone, but the memory of what they did for us is still here and will remain as long as we live.

Another project of Mr. and Mrs. Ford was the restoration of some of the old homes that somehow missed being burned to the ground by Sherman's army during the Civil War. Such homes were Kilkenny, Strathy Hall, and Valambrosia.

Photographs of these are shown elsewhere in this book. These plantations and many others in the area have interesting histories but unfortunately they were destroyed by fire, and otherwise, during the Civil War and thus their recorded family histories were destroyed. When the Kilkenny house was being restored, the carpenters found where a cannon ball had entered the front wall and passed through two more walls of the house. When it was shown to Mr. Ford, he would not let them replace the damaged timbers but had them place a little door there so it could be opened to view the damage that had been done. The house is privately owned today but the small doors are still there. The Kilkenny house had a kitchen separate from the main house. This was the custom then due to the danger of fire. In those days a fire was very serious; there was nothing to fight it with but a few buckets of water. By having the kitchen away from the house, if the kitchen caught fire, there was a good possibility the house could be saved. This old kitchen was also restored and still stands today with the old large fireplace and oven where the food was cooked. This is the only one known to still be in existence in this area. Today the house and kitchen is privately owned.

When Mr. Ford bought Strathy Hall in 1925, the house had been modified many times over the years since it was first built in 1840 and was considerably different from the original structure. I was told by responsible sources at the time that Mrs. Ford was in charge of this restoration. After the restoration, it was lived in by the Bascom Mahaffey family. He was in charge of the plantation garage. Today it is the home of Mr. and Mrs. Neill Baylor. It has been well preserved by the Baylors and is on the National Register of Historic Places.

Another plantation home restored was Valambrosia. The Valambrosia house was in Chatham County across the Ogeechee River from the Ford residence. Little is known about this plantation except that prior to the Civil War, it was a large thriving rice plantation on the north side of the Ogeechee River. It was a large enough operation that they had their own rice mill. Although the Valambrosia property was across the river from the Ford residence, it was quite a long way across the marshes but was still visible from the Ford home so Mr. Ford purchased the property. A photograph of the restored Valambrosia house is shown elsewhere in this book. The house had two floors. The first floor was well up above the ground. This is the way most of the old plantation homes in this area were built back then. They knew that malaria fever was less likely if the house was up off the ground. Of course, we know now that mosquitoes were the cause of malaria fever and the higher the house was off the ground the less mosquitoes there were, and consequently less fever. The house is not standing today but a photograph of the restored house is shown elsewhere.

The Fords did many things that benefited many people in this area over a long period of time, approximately twenty-five years. Many of these were visible things but many of them were invisible things: knowledge, character, independence, self-esteem, and others which cannot be seen or measured. If we hadn't seen these things happen, I'm sure it would be hard for us to believe. We have written about the major things we remember of the Ford days in Richmond Hill. We knew most of the people who lived and worked here during that time. Dates, amounts, quantities, and historical facts were verified from the Richmond Hill Plantation records in the Ford Archives in Dearborn, Michigan. Detailed reports of all activities at Richmond Hill Plantation were sent to Dearborn regularly; some went weekly to the attention of Mr. Frank Campsall, Mr. Ford's personal secretary. If anything warranted Mr. Ford's attention it was given to him or if Mr. Ford asked about something going on down here he was given the information. Telephone conversations between the superintendent here and Mr. Campsall took place as needed. Also, telegrams were sent when mail was too slow to use for communications. Sadly, Mr. Campsall passed away here at Richmond Hill on March 26, 1946, as a result of a heart attack. Mr. Rex Waddell from Dearborn, replaced Mr. Campsall as Mr. Ford's personal secretary.

Some of the photographs are from our own collection which we started when we came to Richmond Hill about sixty years ago. Also, some were given to us over that period. Some we have borrowed from people in Richmond Hill, or who were here during the Ford Era, and have had them reproduced. A large number of the photographs were made by Mr. Ray Newman, a former superintendent of the Plantation. We also obtained photographs from the Ford Archives of the Henry Ford Museum and Greenfield Village in Dearborn, Michigan which are duly identified and credited.

There are some other things we wish we had photographs of, but none are available. However, this large number of photographs will help explain and document some of the many things that Henry and Clara Ford did in the Richmond Hill area. Hopefully, the old saying that "a picture is worth a thousand words" will apply here.

The Henry Ford Era

at *Richmond Hill,* Georgia

HERMITAGE

This old plantation home was located on the banks of the Savannah River. The Hermitage had been the home of Judge Henry McAlphin. It was located adjacent to the Union Bag and Paper Company mill. The property was owned by the Savannah Industrial Development Authority. The Development Authority put the Hermitage up for sale about 1935, when the Fords were making plans for their home. The Fords were advised that the Hermitage was for sale and went and looked at it and bought it. It was not that they wanted their home to be like it but they did like some of its features. They were primarily interested in the "Savannah gray brick" it contained. "Savannah gray brick" were the much-sought-after historic bricks for home construction in the area. They had the home torn down and recovered the brick to build their home at Richmond Hill. The bricks were hauled to Richmond Hill (about 20 miles) and individually hand cleaned for use in constructing their residence. These bricks are of historical significance in the Savannah area because they were made on the Hermitage Plantation prior to the Civil War. Brick making was a major enterprise on this plantation.

FORD RESIDENCE

The Ford residence was the finest structure on the plantation. The site on which the Fords built their home was originally granted to John Harn by the King of England. The original grant was 500 acres and was made in 1748. The second grant was 1,000 acres made in 1758. The large old oak trees on the site appear to be in the shape of an "H" and were probably planted by Mr. Harn. The home Mr. Harn built on the site was called "Dublin" after the family home in Scotland.

The property was passed on to John Maxwell who willed it to his daughter, Mary McIntosh. In 1820 it was sold to Mary Clay who was a descendent of the Reverend Joseph Clay of Boston. The second house built on the site was a rice plantation home called "Richmond". It was burned to the ground during the Civil War. The property remained in the Clay family until 1920 when it was sold to Henry D. Weed of Savannah. Mr. Ford bought the property from Mr. Weed on April 16, 1925.

Mr. and Mrs. Ford apparently spent a lot of time planning their home right down to every detail. Mrs. Ford had a scale model made of it and even had model furniture made for the rooms to give her a better idea of the proportions. That scale model is now on display at the Henry Ford Museum, Dearborn, Michigan.

The first floor had about 3600 square feet and included a living room, dining room, library, kitchen, hallway, storage closets, and ladies and men's restrooms. The hallway was about 10 feet wide and extended from the front door to the back door, a distance of almost 50 feet. Facing the front of the house, the living room was on the left and extended all the way from front to back and was about 25 feet wide and almost 50 feet long plus an alcove of about 250 square feet. Two doors entered the living room, one near the front door and one near the back door. On the right of the hallway at the front was the library which had about 400 square feet. The dining room was on the extreme right side and was about 19 feet wide and 25 feet long. The kitchen was on the extreme right and to the rear. Considerable space off the hallway was devoted to storage closets and men and ladies restrooms. There was a stairway on the left side of the hallway leading to the second floor.

The second floor had about 3300 square feet and included the master bedroom plus five other bedrooms plus the servant's room. The master bedroom had two baths and each of the other bedrooms had a private bath including the servant's room. The hallway on the second floor extended all the way from front to back the same as the first floor. There were several storage closets off the hallway.

The site was perfect for such a wonderful, distinctive, and beautiful residence. The bluff was high and the view out across the Great Ogeechee River was exceedingly beautiful. The lines of oak trees to the front and sides were magnificent. It was perfect in every way for such a distinctive home.

HENRY AND CLARA FORD

This is a rare photograph of Mr. and Mrs. Ford at their Richmond Hill residence. This photo was taken about 1940 at the right front corner of the front porch. The paved walkway to the right led to a circle drive about fifty yards away. No automobiles were ever allowed to be driven up to the house. In the right center background through the trees can be seen the Ogeechee River.

INTERIOR OF LIVING ROOM
OF RESIDENCE

The living room was about 25 feet wide and almost 50 feet long. The fireplace is located about the center of the lengthwise hallway wall. Note the simplicity and the beauty of this portion of the living room. In the opinion of the writers, everything they did at Richmond Hill would fit the category of simple beauty. When the Fords were not in residence. the furniture was draped with muslin covers; even the chandelier had a muslin dust cover. The rugs were rolled up.

Dining Room

The dining room was 19 x25 feet. The chairs appear to be mahogany Philadelphia style Chippendale. We were told the furniture was antique from the Henry Ford Museum in Dearborn. Mrs. Ford was said to have several sets of china, crystal, and silver which were kept in locked closets off the kitchen. The corner cabinet shown here displays some of her choice pieces. The mural wallpaper shows their love of natural scenes. An oriental rug is on the floor. We think we remember that the lighting was indirect.

The Ford Archives has a record of a buffet supper Mrs. Ford had catered by Mrs. Alice Hayward of Savannah Kitchens on February 21, 1939, for 86 guests.

Her menu was:

350 sandwiches consisting of:
shrimp salad
almond and celery
old English cheese
plus
100 toasted peanut butter and bacon
100 rolled Virginia ham paste
100 cheese biscuits

150 cakes to be:
sponge
creole kisses
almond crescents

salted peanuts
small cucumber pickles
mints
coffee, cream, sugar
hot chocolate with whipped cream

DANCING ON LAWN

As previously stated, Mr. and Mrs. Ford had dancing taught at the community house. They occasionally invited students and teachers down to the residence to dance on the lawn. The various quadrilles can be seen dancing. In the quadrille to the right foreground can be seen Mr. and Mrs. Ford. The music was furnished by Mr. Ford's orchestra.

FORD ORCHESTRA

To play the music for the lawn dancing was the Ford orchestra. The versatility of this orchestra was admirable. Mr. Ford can be seen in the center rear conversing with an unknown lady. Mr. Lovett, head of the orchestra, made the calls for the quadrille dances.

ENTRANCE GATE

The entrance gate to the Ford residence was a very simple one. As stated elsewhere Mr. Ford did not care for elaborate things - just simple beauty. This gate fits into that category.

This entrance led to the Cherry Hill plantation house. Turning to the right there, an oyster shell drive led to the Ford residence. You will note there is a small house at the entrance. This was for the gate watchman. Anyone wanting to enter must check with him. A service entrance was located further down the road.

CHERRY HILL

This photo shows the entrance to the Cherry Hill Plantation house. The Fords used this entrance to get to their residence which is about one mile to the right. Mr. and Mrs. Ford stayed in this house when they were here before their home was completed. Also staying at Cherry Hill in an adjacent building when the Fords were here were Mr. Ford's chauffeur, Rufus Wilson, Mrs. Ford's chauffeur, Robert Rankin, and Mr. Ford's secretary, Frank Campsall.

Cherry Hill was a typical southern rice plantation home with live oaks lining the entrance road. The original building was burned during the Civil War. It was rebuilt in 1874 by William Elliot Arnold, son of Richard Arnold. Records at the Henry Ford Museum Greenfield Village archives show that the first deed on record for Cherry Hill was February 1, 1817, in which Mary McIntosh and John Butler deeded the property to Raymond P. Demere, Mary E. Demere and Frances Anne Demere. The next deed was June 5, 1823, in which Sheriff William Hill conveyed the property to Samuel Bond. Bond, in turn, conveyed the property to Richard J. Arnold on December 20, 1824. By the will of Richard J. Arnold, the Cherry Hill Plantation went to his son, William Elliot Arnold, together with other adjoining tracts. This deed was dated January 1, 1874. By a sheriff's deed under foreclosure dated January 1, 1877, the property was conveyed to Paul T. Haskell. The next transaction was by deed on March 25, 1904, in which Paul T. Haskell conveyed the property to Roy A. Rainey. Another deed of December 26, 1919, by Roy A. Rainey conveyed the property to William C. Barnwell and Julian Chisholm. Mr. Ford came into ownership of the property on April 16, 1925.

CHERRY HILL SERVICE BUILDING

This building was located beside the Cherry Hill Plantation House. It had been built by a previous owner but was restored and improved by Mr. Ford. It was here that Mr. Ford's chauffeur, Rufus Wilson, and Mrs. Ford's chauffeur, Robert Rankin, stayed when they were here. Also, Mr. Ford's personal secretary, Frank Campsall, stayed here. Part of the building was used as the plantation office before the office building was constructed at Richmond Hill.

SLAVE CABIN

This slave cabin was located along the entrance road to the Cherry Hill Plantation house. Mr. Ford had it restored. As can be noted it is a nice little cabin. It is only one of many which were originally along the entrance road.

OYSTER SHELL DRIVE

The entrance Mr. and Mrs. Ford used to get to their residence went by the Cherry Hill house. This oyster shell drive continued from Cherry Hill to their residence, a distance of about one mile. At that time oyster shells were abundant in the area and made excellent driveways. There was another entrance to the Ford residence but it was used by workmen and as a service entrance.

OYSTER SHELL DRIVE AT RESIDENCE

This drive was the entrance to the Ford residence. At the far end, a left turn took them to a circle drive near the residence. It is of interest to note that their drive did not go up close to the house but was about 50 yards from it. Apparently, they did not mind walking that short distance. Also, I think they felt that a driveway up to the door would detract from the dignity of the house and I agree. At the end of the drive on the right can be seen a grapevine arbor. In the background to the right can be seen the servant's house. Note the large number of oak trees on the residence grounds adding beauty to the landscape. Through the trees on the far right you can see the Ogeechee River.

VIEW FROM BACK PORCH

As mentioned elsewhere the site the Fords selected for their home was one of the most beautiful of all sites along the great Ogeechee River. The view from the back of the house was just as beautiful as from the front. Note the large river and the beautiful old oak trees along the river bank. This photograph was taken from the back porch. The grass was normally green but due to an unusually cold spell it had turned brown.

SERVANTS HOUSE

This was a very beautiful and unique little house. It was located near the river about halfway between the Ford residence and the powerhouse. It had varnished hardwood floors. Upon entering the front door, on the right was a large sitting room or living room; back of that on the right was a kitchen and dining area. On the left were bedrooms and baths. There was a patio in the back on the river side. It should be pointed out that the chauffeurs, Rufus Wilson (Mr. Ford's chauffeur) and Robert Rankin (Mrs. Ford's chauffeur) did not stay in this house but stayed at the Cherry Hill house as did Frank Campsall, Mr. Ford's secretary.

CHAUFFEURS

Both Mr. and Mrs. Ford had chauffeurs when they were at Richmond Hill. In the top photo is Mr. Robert Rankin, Mrs. Ford's chauffeur. The building in the background is the garage where the automobiles were kept at night. It was located on the residence lawn but obscured from view from the residence by very large oak trees. He is standing beside a Ford but Mrs. Ford usually rode in a Lincoln. The Fords would occasionally ride around on Sunday afternoon. They would ride together in a Lincoln with Rankin driving.

In the bottom photo is Mr. Rufus Wilson, Mr. Ford's chauffeur. Wilson always drove Mr. Ford around the plantation in a Ford – never in a Lincoln. Wilson was a very good driver. I have seen him back that car around between trees by only looking in the rear view mirror. Although Wilson was a chauffeur, he had some authority around the plantation. We were told that Mr. and Mrs. Ford did not call these men "chauffeurs" but referred to them as "drivers."

GARDEN GATE

Mrs. Ford had a garden adjacent to their residence. The gate leading to that garden was one of the most ornate I have ever seen. The craftsmanship here appears perfect. Note that from the center of the gate each side is an exact duplicate of the other except in reverse. Apparently she had it made according to her plans.

MARVIN SHARPE

Mr. Sharpe was caretaker for the Ford residence. He is shown here supervising the covering of one of Mrs. Ford camellia bushes to prevent it from freezing when a freezing temperature was forecasted. Mr. Sharpe did a fine job of taking care of the residence and the grounds. His daughter, Evelyn Phillips, still lives in Richmond Hill.

SLAVE CABIN AT RESIDENCE

T his slave cabin was on the grounds when Mr. Ford purchased the property in 1925. This photograph is believed to have been taken about 1939. It seems impossible, but true, that this cabin had survived since the Civil War. Note the other chimney and the base of another where cabins once stood. The great Ogeechee River is in the background.

RICHMOND NURSERY

Beside the shell drive road between Cherry Hill and the Ford residence a small nursery was maintained. This nursery consisted of large plants which Mrs. Ford might want around the residence. Sometimes large plants in which she was interested were not commercially available. The nursery was near the residence for her convenience so she could choose the kind and size of plant she wanted. Another nursery was maintained near the greenhouse at Richmond Hill which contained smaller plants.

FENCE WITH CHEROKEE ROSES

Mr. and Mrs. Ford's taste in simple beauty was amazing. They had miles and miles of this kind of fence. This particular fence ran from Richmond Hill to Sterling Creek a distance of about two and one-half miles. It had Cherokee roses on it all the way. I don't know who came up with the idea of this kind of fence but it certainly was unique, simple and beautiful. The posts were made of concrete with five rectangular holes evenly spaced to accommodate the fence boards. No joints could be seen in the fence since the boards met in the middle of every other post. The fence and the posts were painted white. The Cherokee rose flower was white and, of course, foliage evergreen. The Cherokee rose is the Georgia state flower. The combination of the white fence, green foliage, and white roses was a beautiful sight to behold. The roses were in full bloom in the spring when the Fords were here. When the Fords were driving from Richmond Hill toward the entrance to their home, they drove this dirt road with the fence and Cherokee roses beside it as shown here.

I am often asked how they could paint the fence with all those roses on it. It was simple. Workmen with gloves would unwind the vine from the fence and lay it down on the ground. The fence would then be painted and when dry the rose vines were put back in place on the fence. This was done each year in the winter before the Fords were expected. A lot of work went into maintaining the fence and roses but it was a thing of beauty.

PETER WILLIAMS

Mr. Ford was almost fanatical concerning tidiness and cleanliness. Peter Williams' sole job was to keep the Richmond Hill area free of paper and trash. Peter was a very faithful worker and did a good job. Thanks to Peter, you would very seldom ever see even a scrap of paper lying around. Also, the people of Richmond Hill were very conscious of cleanliness and were careful not to litter. School children were taught not to throw down paper anywhere in the school building or on the grounds.

FRED MITCHELL

I'm sure you know that Mr. Ford wanted everything kept neat and clean. Here, in the photo at the top right, Fred Mitchell rakes leaves at Cherry Hill. In the background are piles of leaves that have already been raked up. These will be hauled away. The Cherry Hill Plantation house was about one mile from the residence but the Fords always drove by there when going or coming from their residence. For this reason the grounds were always kept looking nice and clean.

TOM BURKE

Tom Burke was one of the gardeners at Cherry Hill. Mr. Ford always wanted everything kept neat and clean. Here Burke rakes up leaves on the Cherry Hill grounds to be removed to make a neat appearance.

RUINS OF OLD RICE MILL

When the Fords bought Richmond Plantation the remains of the old rice mill were still there. However, some cleanup had been done when this photograph was taken in 1930. Prior to the Civil War, all the rice grown on Richmond Plantation was milled in this building. It contained two steam boilers and a steam engine. In cleaning out the debris, the workmen found the old steam engine that had been used to mill the rice. Mr. Ford had this engine put on a railroad flatcar, shipped to Dearborn, and reconditioned and put back into like-new condition. It was shipped back to Richmond Hill and was used to pull the electric generator that generated electricity for the residence.

RESTORED RICE MILL

The restored rice mill was used as a powerhouse to supply utilities to the residence. Two steam boilers were installed and the old rice mill engine that had been reconditioned in Dearborn was put in place. An electric generator was shipped down from Dearborn. It was an old one and apparently had been used in the Ford plant at one time and probably became obsolete for that purpose. Anyway, the steam boilers, the steam engine, and the generator combined to furnish electricity to the residence. Also installed were two V-8 motors each of which was connected to an electric generator. When the boilers were not fired, the engines could be used alternately to generate electricity for the residence.

A word about the reconditioned steam engine seems appropriate. One of my responsibilities was to chemically treat the water used by the steam boilers to prevent scaling. Therefore, I frequently visited the powerhouse. I have stood beside that old engine many times and watched it run in amazement. It was the quietest running steam engine I have ever observed. You could stand within a foot of the flywheel and feel the breeze from it but you could not hear the engine running. The only thing you could hear was the hissing sound of the steam going through the engine. How the Dearborn mechanics ever made it run that smoothly and quietly I'll never know. However, I feel sure they knew Mr. Ford would be listening to the engine and maybe that prompted a super job. Upstairs in the powerhouse he had a jeweler's desk. I was told that he occasionally worked on watches there. Apparently it was relaxing to him.

FIRING THE STEAM BOILER

Henry Carpenter is shown firing one of the steam boilers. The powerhouse was kept immaculately clean. At the far left foreground can be seen part of one of the V-8 engine/generators. In the left far background can be seen part of the other one. Note the white cabinets in the far left center. These were never allowed to become dirty.

MR. FORD AND CHILDREN

Mr. Ford seemed to always enjoy showing the school children around the plantation. Here he is showing them how the steam boiler is fired at the powerhouse at his residence. He is explaining that the steam boiler produces steam to operate the steam engine that pulls the generator to produce electricity.

POWERHOUSE SIDE VIEW
OLD RICE MILL

This photo was taken after Mr. and Mrs. Ford had passed away and the plantation had sold. The unkempt lawn attests to that fact. Such would never have happened in their lifetime.

It is of interest to point out the significance of this old and very tall chimney. There is an underground tunnel leading from the steam boilers inside the building to the chimney. At the base of the chimney there are steps that lead several feet below ground. In the bottom part of the chimney there is a place to build a fire. In rice milling days a fire was started in the bottom part of the chimney. After the fire had been burning for a while, and the heat going up the chimney, it created a suction in the tunnel. The boilers were then fired and the smoke was drawn from the boilers through the tunnel and up the chimney. This design was a very clever one and demonstrates the ingenuity of the early rice planters. At that time steel smoke stacks were not readily available, certainly not as we know them today. Therefore, it was essential to devise a means of creating a suction on the boiler fire and remove the smoke. It also had the effect of making the fire burn faster thus creating more heat and consequently more steam per unit of time.

TUNNEL

This tunnel led from the powerhouse to the residence, a distance of approximately 1100 feet. Through this tunnel ran the electricity, heat, and water for the residence. It was about six feet high and about six feet wide. At the residence there was an elevator to get from the tunnel to both floors.

OYSTER HOUSE

This house was located adjacent to the residence grounds and near the powerhouse. It was called the oyster house because it was built for roasting oysters. The story goes that on a Monday morning Mr. Ford told the superintendent, Mr. Gregory, that he had company coming on Saturday and wanted to roast oysters but did not have a place to do so. On Tuesday they began work on this house and on Saturday they roasted oysters in the fireplace in it. It shows the speed with which things can be done in an all-out effort. Though it may seem impossible to some people to do something that fast, it did not surprise any of us here who worked for Mr. Ford. When he told you to do something he meant now – not later.

Another interesting note about the oyster house was the sign over the entrance door. It read "AIGROEG." All who saw it were mystified by it and wondered what in the world that name could be. They didn't even know how to pronounce it much less what it meant. The puzzle was solved when someone figured out it was Georgia spelled backwards. I don't know whose idea it was to put that sign or label over the door but I will always believe it was Mr. Ford's. Regardless, it certainly was an interesting conversation piece.

WILD TURKEYS ON RESIDENCE LAWN

Mr. Ford believed in the preservation of wildlife and there was plenty of it on the plantation. He had some of the employees put out feed on the lawn for the turkeys every morning. One of the employees was fortunate enough to have snapped this photo early one morning showing the turkeys on the lawn. These are not domestic turkeys but are wild turkeys that have come to the feed on the lawn. Occasionally conversations are overheard that are very interesting. The story is told that one day Mrs. Ford told Mr. Ford to have one of the workmen kill a turkey to have for dinner. He reportedly answered, "No way – If you want a turkey, send to Savannah and get one. They are not going to kill one of my turkeys."

MARTHA-MARY CHAPEL

This is a very impressive structure. It was called Martha-Mary Chapel in honor of Mr. and Mrs. Ford's mothers. Her mother's name was Martha and his mother's name was Mary. The Fords built five other chapels but this is the largest and I think most will agree it is the most beautiful. It is constructed of wood produced here on the plantation. It has a room on each side of the building to the rear. The one on the right is not in view but is identical to the one on the left. These rooms were used by program participants. The chapel would seat about 250 including the balcony. The pews were made of very wide boards and painted white except for some trim which was nicely varnished. There was very nice blue padding on the seats. All the floors were highly varnished hardwood. At the left in the front was a podium for participants. The pews, chairs, and table were made in the plantation cabinet shop. A beautiful crystal chandelier hung in the center.

Note the proximity of the school in the left background. Each school morning there was a 30-minute devotional conducted at the chapel before classes started. In the photo the children can be seen returning to the school. The community house is located to the right adjacent to the chapel. Thus, the school, chapel, and community house were located in close proximity for the convenience of the students.

The school devotionals were conducted by the students under the supervision of the teachers. Each grade took turns for a week at the time. The students walked over from the school and returned informally. The students were seated in the chapel by grades. The teachers usually sat in the balcony. Mr. Ford furnished an organist and the school music teacher taught choruses who sometimes performed. Mr. Ford attended the chapel devotional quite often when they were in residence and Mrs. Ford attended occasionally. When they attended, they sat in the balcony on the right side. Today the chapel is owned by St. Anne's Catholic Church.

In the early Ford era, there was only one denominational church in what is now the city limits of Richmond Hill. It was Canaan Baptist Church, a predominately black church, located at what is now Ford Avenue and Pinecrest Street. It was organized in 1916. The present structure was built in the early Ford era and was partially and indirectly financed by Mr. Ford. There was the Bryan Neck Presbyterian Church in the Keller community about ten miles east of Richmond Hill that was organized in 1830.

MARTHA-MARY CHAPEL

RICHMOND HILL, GEORGIA

APRIL 26, 1942

CHAPEL PROGRAM

PSALM 95

O come, let us sing unto the LORD: let us make a joyful noise to the rock of our salvation.

Let us come before his presence with thanksgiving, and make a joyful noise unto him with psalms.

For the LORD is a great God, and a great King above all gods.

In his hand are the deep places of the earth: the strength of the hills is his also.

The sea is his, and he made it: and his hands formed the dry land.

O come, let us worship and bow down: let us kneel before the LORD our maker.

For he is our God; and we are the people of his pasture, and the sheep of his hand. To day if ye will hear his voice,

Harden not your heart, as in the provocation, and as in the day of temptation in the wilderness:

When your fathers tempted me, proved me, and saw my work.

Forty years long was I grieved with this generation, and said, It is a people that do err in their heart, and they have not known my ways

PRELUDE -- Arioso   Handel

DOXOLOGY

HYMN 184 -- When The Roll Is Called Up Yonder
                                        Stanzas 1, 2, & 3

LORD'S PRAYER

RESPONSIVE READING

HYMN 36 -- Yield Not To Temptation   Stanzas 1, 2, & 3

SCRIRTURE -- Mr. Leslie Long

DUET -- Betty Jean Thomas & Carolyn Mitchum

HYMN 41 -- Love Divine   Stanzas 1, 2, & 4

READING -- Miss Lucy Bunce

HYMN 32 -- O Jesus, I Have Promised   Stanzas 1, 2, & 4

POSTLUDE -- Where God Hath Walked   Mehul

CHAPEL PROGRAM

This is a typical Martha-Mary Chapel program for the community Sunday worship service. The chapel was used by the school every school day and on Sunday by the community. The service was non-denominational. This was the program for April 26, 1942. The programs were printed in the Industrial Arts and Trade School print shop. The organ in the chapel was a very nice one and, of course, furnished by Mr. and Mrs. Ford. The organist changed over the years but at this time was Mrs. Faye Humphery. The service was formal and very impressive. The community appreciated very much the opportunity given them by Mr. and Mrs. Ford to hold their Sunday service in such a fine chapel. The Sunday service was led by someone in the community – a different person each Sunday. A Sunday School was held at 10:00 a.m. prior to the 11:00 a.m. service.

RICHMOND HILL SCHOOL
IN THE EARLY 1930's

This photo of the Richmond Hill School was made in 1938. The year of its construction is not known but probably in the early 1930's. The people in the then Ways Station area floated a bond to construct the building to replace a one-room school which had only six grades. After the school was built, eleven grades were taught; there were two grades in each room. There were two school buses which brought children to school who lived farther than three miles. The buses ran east to the communities of Keller and Bryan Neck, west to the community of Clyde, and south down U. S. Highway 17. The children brought their lunch. This information is from the Reminiscences of Mrs. Harry Gill and is in the Ford Archives at Dearborn, Michigan. Mrs. Gill was a long time resident of Richmond Hill who came here a number of years before the Fords bought land here. She said her son walked to and from school each day, a total distance of about six miles.

RICHMOND HILL CONSOLIDATED SCHOOL
AFTER FOUR-ROOM ADDITION

This photograph was taken in 1940 after Mr. and Mrs. Ford had added four rooms, two on each end, to the building in late 1938 and early 1939. On the right front was a chemistry and physics laboratory which was considered to be the best equipped high school laboratory in the state of Georgia. The school was administered by a County Board of Education and a local Board of Trustees with Mr. Ford's approval. Mr. Ford paid expenses for maintenance, furnished buses and drivers to transport students, furnished free lunches to students and teachers, furnished janitors, supplemented teachers salaries, and many other supplementary services. The building was heated by a coal furnace with radiators in each room. Previously it was heated by a wood heater in each room. He also constructed outdoor tennis and basketball courts.

RICHMOND HILL SCHOOL AUDITORIUM

In terms of today, this may not seem to be anything extra in an auditorium but in the 1930's it was considered to be very advanced as compared to other schools of the area. It easily seated 300. Note the painted scenery. On each side is depicted the great Ogeechee River. Above the stage is a branch of the river with docked boats. There were several backdrops for the stage. The one shown here is a stone fence and the entrance to a garden. All of these extras were made possible by the financial assistance of Mr. and Mrs. Ford. Clarence Smith was principal of the school at this time and had a very good working rapport with Mr. Ford and apparently could get whatever he wanted or needed for the school. This photo was made in 1938 while Mr. Smith was principal.

MOVIE PROJECTOR
IN SCHOOL AUDITORIUM

Today a projector does not look anything like this but this one was modern in the 1930's. It projected a series of actual film photos at the rate of twenty-six frames per second which made the motion seem continuous. The human eye can only detect about half that many frames per second thus it appears continuous. The projector was mounted in an upstairs booth at the rear of the auditorium. In the right bottom foreground is a turntable for playing records to furnish music through the system when desired such as at intermission. At the left can be seen a microphone for making announcements and also a colored light projector. It was used when various colors were desired to be projected onto the stage during stage productions. This photo was made in 1938.

This equipment is obsolete today but the point is that Mr. Ford provided all these things which were modern at the time to make sure that the Richmond Hill students had the best of everything for learning. I personally ran this projector many nights to show the students and parents movies that were available. These were educational movies and I was glad that I could help in this phase of their education. When my wife, Lucy, was teaching she was audio-visual coordinator for all the teachers. She secured film which would be helpful in their teaching and ran the projector. The films were available through the State Department of Education.

WAYS SCHOOL STUDENT COUNCIL

This photo was taken in the Fall of 1938. At that time the name of Ways Station had not been changed to Richmond Hill. That didn't occur until May 1, 1941.

As stated elsewhere, the Ways school was an excellent school in many ways. A great deal of the credit goes to Mr. Ford for his tremendous financial support. Also, there was a fine group of students who were appreciative of what Mr. Ford was doing for them and realized the excellent education they were getting. Shown here is the Student Council for the 1938-39 school year. They are: Front row, left to right, June Davis, Brunelle Smith, Peggy Speir. Back row, left to right: Cecil Rahn, Eldred Hodges, W.J. Logan, Fillmore Gill, Bill Eidson, William Gregory.

1937 GRADUATING CLASS

In addition to all the many wonderful things Mr. and Mrs. Ford did for the school and the students, they sent the graduating senior classes on a trip to Dearborn. This began in 1937 and continued until World War II. Robbie Thomson, office manager, drove the Ford school bus up there and back. The 1937 class was saving their money and conducting fund raisers to go on a trip to Washington, D.C. They were having a meeting at the community house and Mr. Ford came and asked them if they would like to go to Dearborn. They said yes that would be great, but he didn't tell them he was going to pay the bill so they continued to work and make money for the trip. When the time came to go, Mr. Ford had the bus ready with Mr. Thomson the driver. They found out that overnight reservations had already been made and that Mr. Ford was paying for it and it was not going to cost them anything. These overnight reservations were made at very nice places - places that could not be afforded by the students. The students got together and told Mr. Ford they would be glad to pay part of the expenses but Mr. Ford said no, they could use their money for spending money and would not let them pay for any of the trip. While they were in Dearborn they stayed at the Dearborn Inn, an exceptionally nice place to stay. This photo was made in front of the Martha - Mary Chapel at Dearborn in Greenfield Village.

FOUR OF THE RICHMOND HILL TEACHERS

There were numerous school teachers over the years at the Richmond Hill School but this photo made in 1939 of four of them, is the only one available. Left to right are: Fulton Bell, Instructor and Head of Industrial Arts and Trade School; Vivian Williams, Home Economics; Rachael Partain; and Mary McLeod. The Richmond Hill teachers were a very select group. There were several reasons. One reason was the outstanding school system and another reason was that in addition to state and county pay, Mr. Ford supplemented their salary.

RICHMOND HILL SCHOOL LUNCHROOM

M r. Ford built this lunchroom for the Richmond Hill School in the late 1930's. This photo shows only a portion of the lunchroom. There is another section to the left. At that time no other schools in the area had lunchrooms. A few schools had what they called a "soup kitchen" but nothing like a lunchroom. He not only built the building but he furnished all the equipment, supplies, and staff, and gave free lunches to all students and teachers. The students were taught proper behavior and manners while having a meal.

COOKING AREA OF
RICHMOND HILL SCHOOL LUNCHROOM

During the summer when school was not in session the lunchroom crew kept busy canning and preserving fruits and vegetables for use during the school year. The vegetables were grown on the plantation and furnished to the lunchroom. In the photo, left to right are: Vergie Barber, Pearl Carpenter, who was in charge of the lunchroom, Ernestine Sikes, and Jessie Harris.

INTERIOR OF LUNCHROOM

This shows the interior of a section of the lunchroom. The children are well behaved and as you see they are being supervised by teachers. The children were taught good table manners. Also, the boys were taught to pull out the chairs for the girls and to seat them before they could be seated. It was strictly enforced.

Note the neat appearance of everything in the room. The tables and chairs were made in the Ford cabinet shop.

LUNCHROOM WORKERS

This shows another section of the lunchroom where the tables are being set for another group of students. The ladies working here are: left to right, Harriett Jenkins, Ernestine Sikes, and Virgie Barber.

RICHMOND HILL HIGH SCHOOL

GLEE CLUB

In the early nineteen forties, neither state nor county funds were available for music, glee clubs, choruses, or bands. Thanks to the financing of Mr. and Mrs. Ford such things were available to the Richmond Hill High School. Shown here is Miss Anne Wilson, far left, teacher and her glee club. She taught these students and discovered a great deal of talent. Miss Wilson is living in nearby Savannah today where she still teaches piano. Her enthusiasm and interest in students has not diminished. Recently there was a reunion of the 1940's classes in Richmond Hill which she attended. After fifty years she gathered together some of her previous students and they sang some of their old songs for those attending. It was a great hit.

Those shown in this photograph, from left to right are: *First Row* – Betty Findley, Evelyn Smith, Margaret Glynn, Jackie Simmons, Evelyn Strickland, Kitty Cheeves, Winnie Mae Eason, Wilma Harden, Reba Davis, Juanita Shuman, Lillie Davis. *Second Row* – Anne Wilson, Teacher, Wilda Findley, Jeanne Hipp, Jerry Hipp, Cecelia Harvey, Nan McCallar, Freida Speir, Mildred Smith, Lois Williams, Margaret Clark, Louise Moore, Lula Phillips, Gertrude Davis. *Third Row* – Mary Gill, Beth Ann Sharpe, Evelyn Carpenter, Betty Darieng, Betty Jean Thomas, Helen McCallister.

BAND

This photograph was made on graduation night in 1946. The band played as part of the graduation program.

Pictured are: Back row, left to right, standing: Mr. William J. S. Deal, Band Teacher, Margaret Glynn, Jeanne Hipp, Winnie Mae Eason, Betty Zettles, Nan McCallar, Bertie Lee Carpenter, Woody Judy, Johnny Dukes, Laurence Davis, Helen McCallister, Ira Womble, Fulton Mahaffey, Evelyn Carpenter, Jerry Hip. Front row left to right, seated: Mary Gill, Cecelia Harvey, Beth Ann Sharpe, Evangeline Maples, Doris Dukes, Lois Williams, Allen Womble, Dale Mitchum, Jackie Simmons, Betty Darieng.

Mr. Deal came to Richmond Hill when he was released from the army. His wife, Matsy, was teaching an elementary grade here. Before going into the army he had been a band instructor at Statesboro High School and at Georgia Teachers College at Statesboro (now Georgia Southern University).

There were band instruments at the Richmond Hill School not being used as they had no instructor during the war years. The band instruments were bought and a band begun in 1940. Mr. Ted Booker the instructor for band and for music appreciation for all school classes and he had a chorus. All this was paid for by Mr. Ford since the state at that time did not pay for those things. Mr. Booker went into the army early in the war and the band was discontinued as no instructor was available. After 1947, again the band was discontinued when the plantation was cutting expenses.

RICHMOND HILL TEACHERAGE

Mr. Ford built this teacherage for the teachers who taught at the Richmond Hill School. It was located only a short block from the school. It accommodated all the teachers who wanted to live there. Most of the married teachers had their own homes or lived in a Ford built home on the plantation. Any extra space accommodated single Ford employees. During World War II some civilian army personnel who worked at nearby Fort Stewart stayed there. At one time as many as fourteen people lived there. The teachers stayed there at a very reasonable price of $36 per month. Three meals a day were served to the occupants. However, some were not there for the noon meal. The teachers, of course, ate the noon meal at school on Monday through Friday. There was one exception to the three meals a day in that no meal was served on Sunday evenings. However, sandwiches were usually available. The teacherage was staffed by a supervisor, cooks, and maids.

INDUSTRIAL ARTS AND TRADE SCHOOL

This building was constructed in the late 1930's. Mr. Ford, of course, was very much interested in the schools and particularly in the practical side of education. This was built for the students of the Richmond Hill School. The Trade School was located sufficiently close to the school so that the students could easily walk there for their training courses. Classes for adults were available at night.

The Trade School was equipped with necessary equipment for teaching and training in: machine woodwork, bench woodwork, wood and metal finishing, sheet metal work, ornamental iron work, machine shop forging, welding, printing, mechanical and architectural drawing, brass foundry, carpentry. Students from the ninth grade were required to take shop. In the tenth and eleventh grade it was elective. Almost all the tenth and eleventh graders chose to continue their shop training. Boys could work in the shop on Saturday at 12 1/2 cents an hour giving them a chance to earn a little spending money they otherwise would not have. They could also work for an hour or two after school and full days in the summer. Some of the boys who went through the program were able to get very good jobs in industry after finishing school.

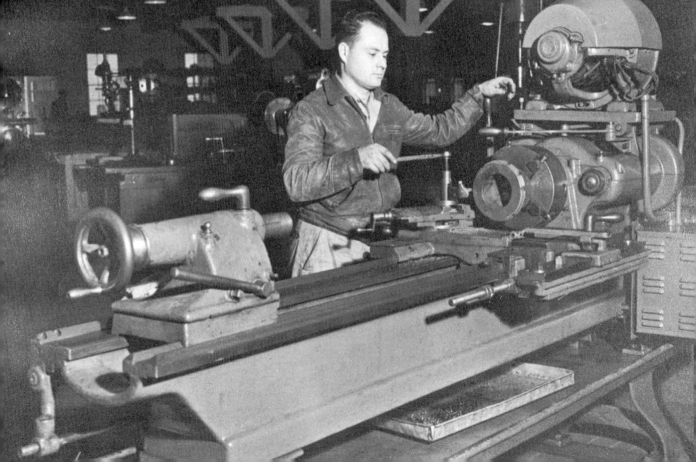

INTERIOR OF INDUSTRIAL ARTS & TRADE SCHOOL

This photo shows a portion of the lathe section of the trade school. In the foreground can be seen a large lathe being operated by Fred Bashlor who specialized in lathe operation. Back of him is Jasper Davis operating a smaller lathe. Back of him is "Bo" Smith operating another machine. To the far right is the instructor in charge of the trade school, Fulton Bell.

CLOSE-UP OF LARGE LATHE

This lathe is being operate by Fred Bashlor. He started in the trade school as a student and became an expert in lathe operation. He later was employed by a large company in nearby Savannah, Georgia at a very good salary. This is an example of the value of the training received in the Ford Trade School. All of this, of course, was made possible by the generosity of Henry Ford. Mr. Bashlor is now retired and lives in the Savannah area.

A Portion of The Industrial Arts and Trade School

Five students are shown operating machines in a portion of the trade school. In the far right background can be seen the head and shoulders of Fulton Bell, instructor and head of the trade school. In the left background is the print shop and drafting room. Miss Mary Rogers taught printing. The print shop printed various forms for the plantation and programs for school functions and the Sunday programs for Martha-Mary Chapel.

COMMUNITY HOUSE

This was the most prestigious of all Ford buildings in Richmond Hill except the Ford residence. It was built in 1936. The value of the educational and cultural advancement that was received in this building cannot be overstated.

A word about the floor plan may be helpful to the reader. The front of the building is to the right. Facing the front, on the left is the spacious living room. On the right front is the dining room. Upstairs on the front is a very large ballroom. On the right back of the dining room was a very large kitchen. Between the front section and the back section were ladies' lounges and men's restrooms. Note that in the far left there is an entrance to the rear section of the building. In this section there was the hostess' suite plus numerous class rooms for teaching home economics. There were rooms for instruction, and sewing room with several sewing machines. Cooking was taught in the large kitchen. Upstairs were bedrooms for the home economics students. Each class of home economics students spent a week at the Community House on a rotational basis. They were taught everything from how to make up a bed to all the social graces. They were taught how to plan a meal, how to shop for the ingredients, how to prepare the meal, and how to serve it according to accepted etiquette standards. The ingredients were obtained at the Ford Commissary. Although called a commissary, it was more than that. It was also a very good grocery store carrying an excellent quality of groceries. They also had a very good meat department. All of the groceries for the Home Economics Department were furnished by Mr. and Mrs. Ford at no cost to students or parents. All of the school functions were held in the Community House. One particularly important function was the Junior-Senior Banquet. All the Community House, including the ballroom, was elaborately decorated and the students were dressed in their finest. There was absolutely no misbehavior. Such good behavior was almost unbelievable. They did not walk across the dance floor but around it. They did not chew gum. Their table manners were exceptional. Though young, I think the students realized the valuable training they were getting at no cost to them or their parents and they appreciated it. Also, the parents deserve a great deal of credit for the discipline and training the students received at home. I called the Community House "The Cultural Center of Richmond Hill" and truly it was. After more than fifty years the results of the training these young ladies received in the Community House is still evident. Although admittedly an exaggeration, I have often said I can pick out every lady in Richmond Hill who went through that training. I'm sure you see my point.

The students were taught quadrille dances. Mr. Ford hired a dancing teacher from Savannah, Mrs. Ebba Thomson, to come out once a week and teach these dances to the students in the Community House ballroom. The students soon became quite good at these dances. Mr. Ford had an orchestra, headed by Mr. Benjamin Lovett, that he sometimes brought down from Dearborn when he and Mrs. Ford were here to play for the student dances. Otherwise, the music for the dances was from recordings by the Ford orchestra. I shall never forget attending one of the dancing

demonstrations performed by the young children showing their accomplishments. A young girl was sitting beside me when a young boy came up and bowed to her and asked her to dance. She got up and curtsied after he bowed, and they danced. What a wonderful experience to see the results of Mr. Ford's financed cultural training of these young children. The Community House was also used by adults. If the community wanted to have a party they could have it at the Community House. The adults usually had a Christmas party there. It was decorated to perfection from locally grown material. The large overhead beams in the ballroom were wrapped with ivy and holly with red berries and Christmas lights attached. It was beautiful beyond description. A Christmas dinner was prepared by community ladies. Participants were not limited to Ford employees and non-employees were welcome and participated. It was like a family affair. Dances were usually held in conjunction with the Christmas party.

In later years an adult dancing group was formed and we had a dance at the Community House every month. The music was provided from recording made by the Ford orchestra. The dances were the same quadrilles as taught to the students.

COMMUNITY HOUSE KITCHEN

This photo was made in 1940. This was a very large kitchen with all modern conveniences of that time. In this kitchen is where the home economics students were taught to cook. The students from left to right are: Vardelle Lowery, Elizabeth Lanier, and Georgia Harvey. Note the large four-door refrigerator with nicely finished wooden doors. The work table is stainless steel and the leg extensions support the pots and pans hung above. Of particular interest is the cooking stove on the left. The stove was made in Sweden and burned Pennsylvania nut coal. It needed firing only once every twelve hours and used only about two gallons of coal per day while in use. On the left side of the stove you will see a raised lid and a pot being placed on the stove. The lid was for insulation and was about four inches thick. When you were ready to cook you simply raised the lid and placed the pot on the stove. When finished cooking the lid was lowered back down on the stove. The stove stayed hot and could be cooked on anytime. It also had an oven that stayed hot for baking. It was a remarkable stove. An electric range was also available. All the counters were stainless steel.

There was another section of the kitchen adjacent to the dining room which served somewhat like a butler's pantry. It contained another refrigerator like the one pictured here and cabinets for china, glassware, and other serving utensils.

COMMUNITY HOUSE LIVING ROOM

This photo was made in 1940. Shown here are some of the home economics girls relaxing in the spacious living room of the Community House. They are left to right: (1) Unknown, (2) Doris Burch, (3) LaWanda McCallar, (4) Betty Lou McAllister, (5) Gladys Smith, and (6) Elizabeth Lanier. Each home economics class spent a week at the Community House on a rotational basis. There were sufficient bedrooms to accommodate the students.

LIVING ROOM CONSTRUCTION

The construction of the Community House was far above and beyond the normal quality of construction. Note, for example, the close spacing and size of the ceiling joists. Everything imaginable was done to make it the best.

The stairs in the background lead to the ballroom upstairs. The door to the left leads to a surrounding porch and side entrance. The door in the right background leads down a hall to another perpendicular hall to the left of which is another entrance. The back hall gave entrance to the Home Economics classrooms. Not visible in this photo, but in the far background to the right is a door leading to the entrance hall and the dining room. In the foreground to the right (not visible) is another door leading to the entrance hall.

COMMUNITY HOUSE DINING ROOM

This photograph does not do justice to the dining room but is the only one available. It was taken before all the furniture was in place and before being decorated. When completed it seated about sixty. All school parties were held here including the junior-senior banquets. When adults had parties here some very elaborate meals and refreshments were served. The adults usually had a Christmas party here with all the trimmings including decoration of the ballroom, dining room, and living room. It was a sight to behold.

TEACHER AND STUDENTS IN SEWING ROOM

The Community House had specific rooms set aside for the teaching of home economics. This one was for sewing. From left to right are: Elizabeth Akins, teacher, LaWanda McCallar, Martha Burch, Georgia Harvey, and Gladys Smith.

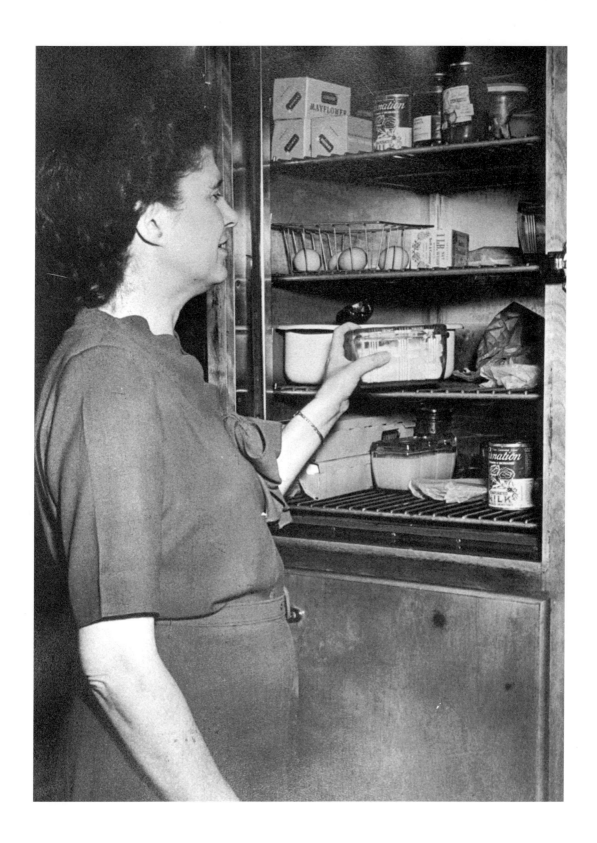

MISS AMBER LEE

Miss Lee is shown here in the kitchen at the large four-compartment refrigerator. She was hostess at the Community House several years prior to its closing after the death of Mr. Ford. She came to Richmond Hill in 1943. In her reminiscences she says she was told that most of the furniture in the Community House was brought down from Dearborn. The chairs in the ballroom were made in the cabinet shop in Dearborn. Mrs. Dahlinger, from Dearborn, helped in the decoration. Miss Lee said groups of school children from other counties in Georgia came to the Community House to see the dancing. Miss Lee recently passed away.

COMMUNITY HOUSE BALLROOM

This picture shows a high school dance class in the early 1940's. There was a small stage next to the back wall where the piano was placed. To the right of the piano, Mrs. Ebba Thomson is directing the dancing. She brought the pianist, whom Mr. Ford paid, with her from Savannah. Teachers are sitting on the stage in the back.

BALLROOM CONSTRUCTION

Some readers may be interested in what the ballroom looked like during construction in 1936. Note that the ceiling and walls are not yet complete. The workmen are preparing the boards for the walls and ceiling. Note the large beams extending from one side of the ballroom to the other. Nothing but the best in materials and workmanship was used.

ROBBIE & EBBA THOMSON

In the early days of the plantation Robbie Thomson was office manager. Later Robbie went into business for himself in Savannah and Ben Brewton became the office manager. Robbie's wife, Ebba, was a dancing and ballet teacher in Savannah. Mr. Ford hired her to teach dancing in the large ballroom of the Community House. The dances were the old fashioned square dances. She usually taught once a week but she came more often when the Fords were here because the Fords wanted to see the students dance. Occasionally Mr. Ford brought his orchestra and Mr. Lovett, the dance master, to Richmond Hill and they would play for the students to dance. When the orchestra was not here Mr. Ford paid a pianist to play for the dance lessons. Records of the orchestra and caller of the dances were available also.

LEARNING THE DANCES

These students are shown learning the quadrille dances in the ballroom of the Community House. At left, Mr. Benjamin Lovett, head of the Ford orchestra, looks on as the orchestra plays for the dances.

DANCING

The Ford orchestra plays for the students to dance in the Community House ballroom. Mr. Ford would often bring his orchestra down to Richmond Hill and have them play for the students to dance. It was something Mr.and Mrs. Ford obviously enjoyed. The members of the orchestra which came to Richmond Hill were: "Little Billy," Perry, Baxter and Castell. Shown here are the students learning ballroom dancing.

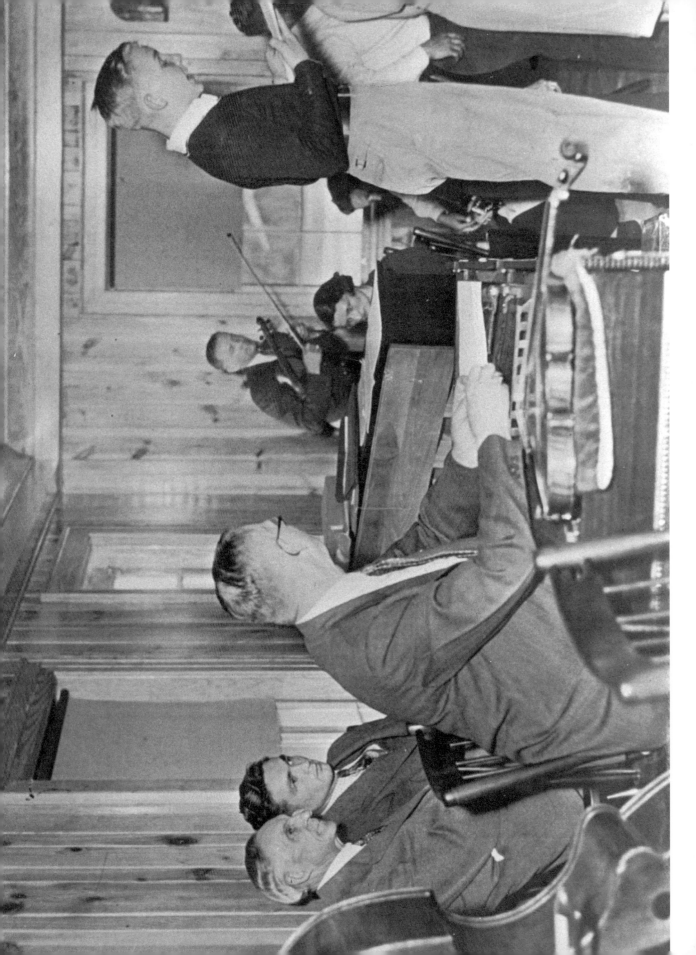

STUDENTS PERFORM FOR MR. FORD

This photo was taken about 1940. As previously stated Mr. and Mrs. Ford were very much interested in teaching students dancing. In this ballroom of the Community House is where the dancing was taught. A lady from Savannah Mrs. Ebba Thomson, was hired by Mr. Ford as the teacher to teach one day a week all during school. Sometimes Mr. Ford brought his orchestra down to play for the students to dance. The orchestra members who usually came down were "Little Billy," Perry, Baxter, and Castel. Mr. Benjamin Lovett headed the orchestra.

In this photo the students are being taught to play the music for the dances. Miss Georgia Harvey is at the piano and G. B. Spence (standing) is doing the calling for the quadrilles. Barely visible behind Spence is a student playing the guitar. At the far left is Mr. Ford. Next to him is Clarence Smith, principal of the Richmond Hill School. In the center to the right, out of view, the students perform the dances for Mr. Ford.

LANDSCAPE POOL

This pool was built across the road from the Community House. It was a very beautiful pool with artistically designed walls curving in and out adjacent to the lovely trees. It was only about three feet deep and not designed for swimming but for beautification. The water was supplied by a six-inch diameter flowing well. The beautiful lady in the photo is Miss Evelyn Carpenter, daughter of Mrs. Pearl Carpenter who was in charge of the school lunchroom.

There is a very interesting story about this pool. I don't know how the pool came to be built but it was built by the plantation with the approval of Mr. Ford. I'm sure Mr. Gregory was proud of this beautiful pool and when the Fords came down he showed it to them. I was told on good authority that Mrs. Ford took one look at the pool and said, "Cover it up." I do know that immediately work was begun on covering it up. I recall seeing numerous dump trucks hauling dirt all day long every day filling it in. In short order it was all filled in and you couldn't tell there had ever been a pool there. I don't know what Mrs. Ford 's objections were but I was told she said it would only raise mosquitoes. Everybody else thought it was beautiful and greatly enhanced the attractiveness of the landscape.

GORDON BUTLER'S STORE

As the plantation was just getting started and before Mr. Ford had built a place to pay off employees, they were paid in this store on Friday afternoon beginning at 4:30. They were paid in cash which had previously been placed in a pay envelope. Each employee had a numbered badge which had to be presented to receive pay. The store was located adjacent to the Seaboard Railroad and convenient to all. This arrangement was good for the plantation and was good for Mr. Butler's business. It was a general type store carrying groceries, dry goods, and some hardware and general supplies. The post office was also located in this store. The rural mail carrier was Mr. Ira Casey, Sr. who delivered the mail to rural areas. The post office had a dozen or so pigeon-holed boxes for mail. When you asked for your mail the clerk would look through the mail to see if you had any.

Later, Mr. Ford bought Gordon Butler's store and a nearby one-room schoolhouse was remodeled for the post office. The store was torn down and the commissary was built across the road. Employees were then paid at the gas department.

FORD COMMISSARY

This photograph of the Ford Commissary is a recent one. A photograph during the Ford era is not available. The Commissary Building was recently purchased by the Community Christian Church. Church services are held there each Sunday. The previous owner of the building had placed a marker above the door which reads: "The Commissary Building - From the Henry Ford Era, circa 1940."

The commissary was built by the Fords and opened in 1941. It was operated by the Ford Plantation for the convenience of the community and not just for the employees. In addition to groceries, it carried some general merchandise – even some dry goods. The groceries were top quality at reasonable prices. This is where the home economics students from the Community House got their groceries and supplies for their training in cooking. All this was furnished free to them by the Fords. The commissary had an excellent meat department. They carried only first quality meats, especially beef and pork. They always employed an excellent butcher who knew his meat and how to cut it. In those days most of beef and pork was delivered to the store in side halves. The butcher did all the cutting into smaller cuts for the customers. During oyster season they carried fresh oysters from the oyster house at Kilkenny. They also carried fresh produce grown on the farm such as Irish potatoes, sweet potatoes, cabbage, beans, peas and corn in season. Over the years there were several managers of the commissary. Some of them were Carl Ramsey, Stuart Carpenter, Jim Elkins, and Dewey Mitchum.

BAKERY

The bakery was built adjacent to the commissary in 1941. It was first simply called the "Bakery" but in later years it was called the "Sweet Shop." Mr. Ira C. Womble was selected to run the bakery. He had been running a bakery in Savannah. He baked a wide variety such as bread, rolls, cakes, pies, cookies, doughnuts, and also made and sold ice cream. His fruitcake was well liked by Mrs. Ford and a supply was sent to Dearborn for Thanksgiving and Christmas each year.

The Sweet Shop made a nice stop for after work and after school sweets. A photograph of the exterior of the building during that time is not available. This photo shows a young student customer making his choice.

POST OFFICE

The post office had previously been in a portion of Gordon Butler's store. This was in the early 1930's. A photo of that store is shown elsewhere. Mrs. Edna Butler, wife of Gordon Butler, was the post mistress, having been appointed June 2, 1930. The amount of mail at that time was very small. The local people would simply go to the store and ask if they had any mail. The post mistress would look through the mail to see if they had any. There was only one rural route. The mail carrier was Mr. Ira C. Casey, Sr.. He delivered mail to outlying communities such as Keller, Belfast, and along U.S. Highway 17. People without post office boxes and not on the rural route received their mail by calling for it at the post office.

When Gordon Butler's store closed in about 1940, a building located adjacent to the bakery was remodeled for a post office. This photo was taken inside that building. Note that on the left there are sixteen boxes. This was the original number in this building. On the right you will note that about one hundred boxes have been added. Today the Richmond Hill post office is a modern building with about 3000 boxes and has eight rural routes.

MR. GREGORY AND STEVE SCREVEN

Steve Screven was one of the plantation workers. He served as "pusher" in one of the labor crews. Steve was not good at managing his money and usually was broke on Monday morning. Here he is shown talking to Mr. Jack Gregory, plantation superintendent, apparently as usual, asking to borrow money until payday. Mr. Gregory looks at his last pay envelope and probably loaned him money as he usually did.

WAYS STATION ABOUT 1938

As previously mentioned, this community was called Ways Station before it was named Richmond Hill in 1941. This is a typical scene around Ways Station about 1938. The Mitchum house is shown in the left center. This is where the Mitchums roomed some of the teachers prior to the Fords building the teacherage. In the far right background can be seen the Richmond Hill School and the white building back of it is the school lunchroom built by Ford. Beyond the Mitchum house beside the road can be seen another house. This house was where Mrs. Molly Gill lived who ran the Bunkhouse and the dining room. Note the road is paved only up to the Atlantic Coastline Railroad.

WAYS RAILROAD STATION

When the Fords bought their property at Ways Station there was very little here. There was, however, a railroad station on the Atlantic Coastline Railroad. When the Fords first began coming down, they came in their railroad car named "Fairlane". This was parked on the sidetrack at this station. In this photo it was parked on the right side of the tracks starting in front of the vehicle and extending to the right out of view in this photo. There was another railroad through Ways, the Seaboard Airline Railway but the Fords used the Atlantic Coastline. I mention this because there is sometimes confusion as to which railroad they used.

The reader may wonder why the name "Ways", so I will attempt to clarify. Railroads often ran through sparsely populated areas but there may have been a need for a station (depot) there. The railroad mostly did the naming and usually named it for some well-known person or thing in the area. In this case there was a Mr. Way who owned a plantation nearby so it was called Ways Station. It was not until May 1, 1941 that the name "Ways Station" was changed to Richmond Hill. By 1941 Mr. and Mrs. Ford had done so much for Ways that the community wanted to do something to honor them. The names "Ford City,""Fordtown," and "Fordville," were suggested but I don't think Mr. Ford wanted his name used like that. The next choice was "Richmond," the name used for their residence which came from an old rice plantation home that had been on the site prior to the Civil War. Changing the name of a town can be a very complicated undertaking. It has to be approved by the state and the United States Postal Service. The name "Richmond" was sent in but apparently there was already a small town with that name in Georgia so it could not be used. Someone then suggested adding "Hill" to the name. That was approved so the name became "Richmond Hill". There is no hill at Richmond Hill but there was a plantation here named "Cherry Hill" and "hill" was occasionally added to plantation names. So Ways Station became Richmond Hill.

THE BUNKHOUSE

This is where single men, who worked for the plantation, boarded who chose to live at Richmond Hill. A few married men also boarded there during the week if they lived further away than they wanted to commute each day. In the left of the photo can be seen the corner of the dining room where the boarders had their meals. The teachers, who roomed with the Mitchums next door, had their morning and evening meals there. At noon, of course, they ate at the school lunchroom. As I recall, these two buildings were the only two inhabited buildings on the plantation that were not painted white.

PLANTATION OFFICE BUILDING

This was a relatively small building with five rooms and two restrooms. There was a room for the superintendent, the office manager, bookkeeper, payroll check, and telephone exchange. I am often asked where was Mr. Ford's office. The truth is he didn't have an office down here. I am sure he didn't come down to Richmond Hill to sit in an office. I don't know what he did elsewhere, but I can tell you he was too interested in all the many things that were going on here on the plantation to sit in an office. He was always on the go - seemed to always be in a hurry. Just think of all the many things he could be doing of interest instead of sitting in an office. For example, he could be visiting the sawmill, Trade School, Community House, Research Laboratory, Richmond Hill School, Carver School, farming operations, just to mention a few. So why in the world would he want to sit in an office. The answer is obvious. He did occasionally go into the superintendent's office and talk with him - apparently on business matters.

RAY B. NEWMAN

M r. Newman was superintendent of Richmond Hill Plantation from 1946 until 1951 when the plantation was sold after the deaths of Mr. and Mrs. Ford. Mr. Newman had been with the Ford farming operations in Dearborn, Michigan. He came to Richmond Hill in April of 1946 after a letter from Mrs. Ford terminated the employment of Mr. Jack Gregory. He and his wife lived in the superintendent's house that was previously occupied by Mr. Gregory and his family.

In Mr. Newman's Reminiscences, he said the Fords interviewed him for the job here. His orders were to cut the overhead and to show a profit. So when he came, some activities of the plantation were curtailed. School operations were returned to the Board of Education.

FIRE TRUCK AND AMBULANCE

These vehicles were kept in the Fire Station Building shown in the background. The Fire Station was near the office, the sawmill, and the Trade School so that, if needed, help would be nearby. In the photo, front, left to right are: Earl Sheppard, Herman Coffer. In the rear, left to right are: Richard Smith, Jasper Davis, and "Bo" Smith.

After the plantation sold, Mr. and Mrs. Jack Phillips bought the Fire Station Building, had it moved, and made into a residence. It is an attractive home today and still has the fireman's brass pole in it.

Bascom Mahaffey

Bascom Mahaffey and his family came to Richmond Hill in 1938. They lived at Strathy Hall, a plantation home that Mr. and Mrs. Ford had restored on the banks of the Ogeechee River. He was in charge of the garage and was responsible for all mechanized mobile equipment including maintenance and repairs. In 1946, there were 55 trucks and cars, 18 Ford-Ferguson tractors, 12 Fordson tractors and 10 school buses according to a list in the Ford Archives in Dearborn, Michigan. In addition, there were bulldozers and draglines.

Mr. Mahaffey went to work with Ford in Jacksonville, Florida, in 1924, where he was employed in various capacities including road service to dealers. He was chosen to come to Richmond Hill because of his varied background and because he had some diesel engine experience. When he came, the garage was located in a shed with a dirt floor. When Mr. Ford asked him if he had some plans for a garage building, Mr. Mahaffey very soon had a good one sketched out as he had helped dealers plan and remodel garages in his road service. The plantation garage was a large building with two sections. In one section, cars and trucks were repaired. Another section was devoted to maintenance and repairs of tractors and other heavy equipment. The garage also had a parts department. Mr. Mahaffey had a number of mechanics and helpers working under him.

Mr. Mahaffey was active in community affairs also. He served as a school trustee. He also served on the War Price and Rationing Board during World War II with Mr. Harry Ukkelberg and Mr. Louis Gill (not a plantation employee).

The Mahaffeys had four children, Elizabeth, Bascom, Jr., and Fulton, who were in school in Richmond Hill in the 1940's. They had a younger son, Ernest, born in 1946. The Mahaffeys were both active in the Parents Teachers Association and the Presbyterian Church. They frequently entertained the school teachers at Strathy Hall. After the plantation closed, Mr. Mahaffey and family moved so he could work at a Ford dealership in Vidalia, Georgia.

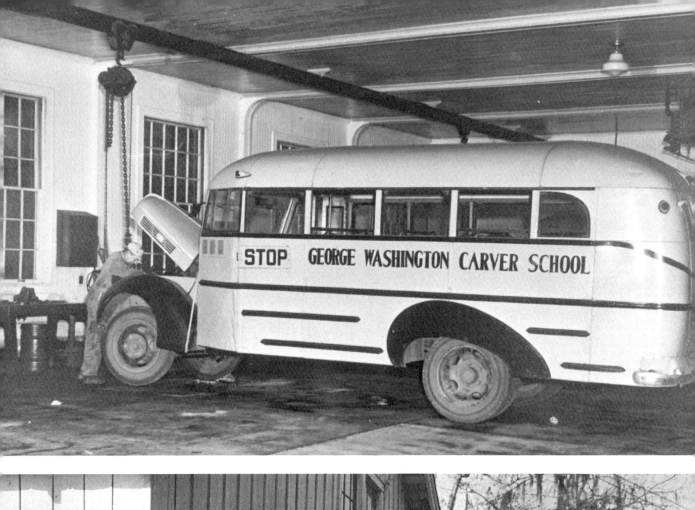

INTERIOR OF GARAGE

The Carver school buses were serviced and repaired in the Ford garage in Richmond Hill. Here Raleigh Davis repairs one of the buses.

GAS DISBURSEMENT

Herman Coffer disburses gas into a station wagon used on the plantation.

GAS DEPARTMENT AND GARAGE

In the center background is the gas department where the cars were refueled. Oil and other supplies were also kept in this building. On the far end of this building was the electrician's shop. Out in front of the building were gas pumps for refueling trucks and tractors. This building was also used to pay employees on Friday afternoon beginning at 4:30. All were paid in cash.

In the right foreground is the corner of the garage. The garage was a large building where cars, trucks, and tractors were serviced and repaired. The garage had a parts department and a paint room. Mr. Bascom Mahaffey was in charge of the garage.

WILLIE "SLIM" GEORGE

"Slim" was the gas attendant at the gas department and kept a record of the gas disbursed to each vehicle. He had a very serious eye problem. Mr. Ford paid for his eye treatment and the eye was surgically removed and Mr. Ford paid for his glass eye.

Mr. Ford and Will Showers

Mr. Ford chats with Will Showers who was the watchman at the entrance to the plantation office. Will had lost part of his right leg in a sawmill accident prior to Mr. Ford coming to Richmond Hill and had a wooden leg. Mr. Ford, in his humanitarian way, gave Will a job at the entrance. There was not a gate at the entrance but there was a small watchman's house. Showers knew practically all who came and went through the entrance, and if a stranger should come by he would know it. Will Showers was a very tall man; note how much taller he is than Mr. Ford.

FORD CLINIC

Mrs. Constance Clark was employed in May, 1930 by Mrs. Samuel Rotan to carry on free health work in lower Bryan County known as "Ways Health Association". Mrs. Clark was furnished a house to live in free by Mrs. Rotan. In May 1935 Mrs. Rotan gave up this program and Mr. Ford assumed the obligation and hired Mrs. Clark to continue the health work. The clinic then was located where the Community House was later built so then this clinic building pictured here was built near the Atlantic Coastline Railroad. This building was larger than it appears in this photograph. There was a waiting room on the left front and a nurses room on the right front. In the back were examining rooms, an office and storage area. Mrs. Constance Clark was the head nurse. Nurse Ella Reed Sams was also on duty. Mrs. Ukkelberg worked some days when the doctors came out.

After the plantation was closed the building was moved and today it is a residence.

WAITING ROOM OF CLINIC

Ella Reed Sams, or "Nurse Reed" as she was affectionately called, stands on the right calling patient from waiting room. Left to right are: Maybelle Demere, unknown, Carrie Maddox. Nurse Reed was an outstanding nurse. Her patience and care for the sick was unexcelled. She lived in Savannah and drove out to Richmond Hill every work day.

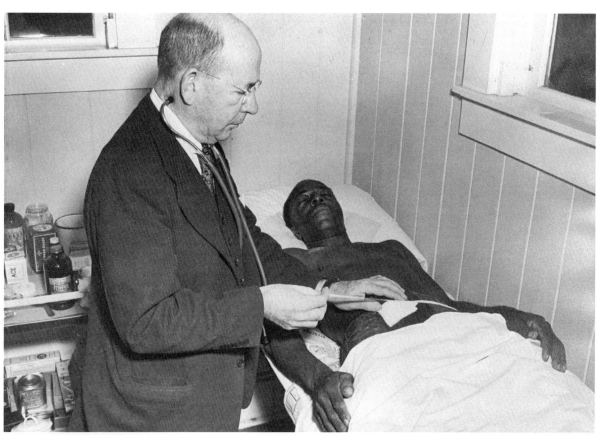
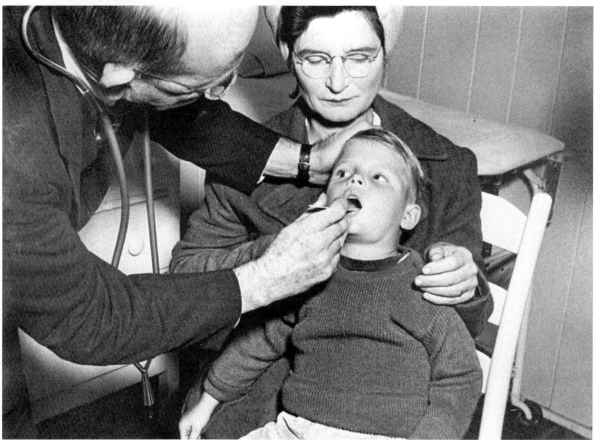

Dr. C. F. Holton and Employee Patient

D r. Holton is shown here examining an employee. It was a great satisfaction to the employees to know that their medical needs were all taken care of by Mr. Ford. They were all very appreciative of what Mr. Ford was doing for them.

Dr. C. F. Holton and Patient

M rs. Maude Sauls Harvey holds her son, James, while Dr. Holton takes a look at his throat. Dr. Holton came from Savannah out to the clinic every Thursday and more often if needed. If for some reason Dr. Holton couldn't come, Dr. John Sharpley came. They had a practice together in Savannah. Any Ford employee was treated free including medicine. Many non-employees in the area were also treated free.

GETTING AN INJECTION

Mrs. Constance Clark, head of the Ford Clinic, gives an injection to a little girl in the countryside near Richmond Hill. In addition to the treatment of patients at the clinic, nurses went out into the rural areas and treated patients. It might be oral medication, injection, immunization, or whatever the case called for. At first some of the patients, or parents of the patients, were somewhat skeptical but after some spectacular results, the skepticism soon disappeared. Note in this photo the intense watchful eyes of onlookers.

FORD KINDERGARTEN IN RICHMOND HILL

This building was constructed in 1940-41 as a model kindergarten for children from three to six years of age. The 3500 sq. ft. building was an attractive home-like bungalow with two large rooms, a kitchen, and a bathroom. In the bathroom, in addition to the regular commode and lavatory, was a small size commode and lavatory especially made for small children. The equipment such as a tables and chairs was made in the Ford cabinet shop. Also built in the cabinet shop were small wooden lockers that lined the walls for the children's belongings. There was a locker for each child. The designs for the equipment were furnished by Kate Baldwin Free Kindergarten at Columbia University in New York. It was considered to be the leading kindergarten in the country and provided for scientific development of children.

Miss Margaret Mustin was appointed to the position of Director upon the recommendation of Kate Baldwin Free Kindergarten. Miss Mustin had an A.B. Degree from Shorter College, Rome, Georgia. She had worked at Shorter College for two years as assistant professor of biology. She studied art in New York at the School of Fine and Applied Arts. She was graduated from Baldwin Normal School in New York and became assistant director of the 49th Street Public School Kindergarten. In the two summers prior to coming to Richmond Hill, she was working toward her Master's Degree in Nursery School, Kindergarten, and First Grade Education at Teachers College, Columbia University.

After coming to Richmond Hill, she continued her studies there in the summer. Mr. Ford is believed to have paid her expenses there. It is evident that the Fords were interested in getting the best qualified director possible for the kindergarten at Richmond Hill. It was evident that Miss Mustin was doing a great job at the kindergarten at Richmond Hill.

Miss Mustin left Richmond Hill in 1944 to be married to a serviceman. In 1945 Mrs. Willie Newton Bennett became head of the kindergarten and was assisted by Annie Ridgell and Evelyn Phillips. Lulie Poinsett also worked there.

The number of children attending the kindergarten ranged from 25 to 40. They were either brought to the kindergarten by their parents or picked up at home by one of the employees of the kindergarten. A station wagon was furnished to the kindergarten for their use by Mr. Ford.

A full meal was served to the children at noon. After lunch there was a rest period with cots being provided for each child. The children were dismissed at 2:30 p.m. They were either picked up by their parents or taken home by kindergarten employees. There was no charge to the parents of the children. In fact, they did not even have to be employees of the Ford Plantation.

After the plantation closed, some of the equipment and supplies was given to the Methodist Church and some to the Baptist Church. After the plantation was sold to International Paper

Company, the kindergarten building was converted into offices. Today it is owned by Magnolia Manor, a retirement home owned by the Methodist Church. Magnolia Manor kindly allows the Richmond Hill Historical Society to use the building.

MISS MARGARET MUSTIN

This lady was head of the Richmond Hill Kindergarten from its beginning until 1945. She is shown here with one of her students, Rebecca Gill. The vehicle is a station wagon, a Ford of course, she used to pick up the children in the morning and take them home in the afternoon.

INTERIOR OF FORD KINDERGARTEN

This photo shows only a small portion of the kindergarten. However, it does show something about the arrangement, equipment, and activity. The tables and chairs were built in the Ford cabinet shop. Also in the center rear can be seen some of the small child-sized lockers that were also built in the Ford cabinet shop. There were many more lockers, enough for each child to have one. Note the square tables that accommodated four children, as modern as today even though more than fifty years later. Also note there are rectangular tables on the left and an easel on the right for drawing. In the center right note the doll-size bed. As you see, everything imaginable was provided for these children and gave them an atmosphere conducive to learning.

There are some in Richmond Hill today who recall their days in the Ford Kindergarten with a great deal of pleasure and appreciation. The teachers, left to right, are: Mrs. Ted Booker and Mrs. Willie Bennett, Director.

COURTHOUSE

Mr. Ford recognized the need for a building in which to vote and hold community business meetings. He built this building in 1939 and it began to be called the courthouse although it was never used as a courthouse. The county courthouse was at Pembroke, the county seat of Bryan County. The building was used as a voting place for the Richmond Hill area. Area business meetings were held there. Also holding meetings there were the Masonic Lodge and the Order of Eastern Star. Today the upstairs is used for offices of the City of Richmond Hill. Part of the downstairs is used by the Tax Commissioner of Bryan County. Also downstairs is a community meeting room.

BAILEY CARPENTER

When Henry Ford came to Richmond Hill, Bailey Carpenter was a 29-year old barber. His shop was a very small wooden building and was located in Richmond Hill. (then Ways Station) at the intersection of U.S. Highway 17 and State Highway 144. It was the only barber shop in Richmond Hill.

One day Mr. Ford walked into the shop and said to Bailey, "Young man I'd like for you to cut my hair, and when you are finished, I want you to shave me." No doubt, many barbers would have been nervous giving Henry Ford a haircut and shave, but Bailey says he was just another guy. The going rate for a haircut and shave in the late 1930's was 35 cents. After the haircut and shave, Mr. Ford handed him an envelope. When Bailey went home that evening he opened the envelope and found that Mr. Ford had given him ten dollars. That was the same amount that Carpenter was paying per month for rent.

Soon afterwards, Mr. Ford offered to move Bailey's shop to a location more convenient for him and Mr. Ford. He told Carpenter, "I'll get you a cheaper place." He said "I'll give you free rent down there by the school, and I'll have my men move you there." So Mr. Ford had his shop moved.

One day the plantation superintendent, Mr. Jack Gregory, went to Carpenter's barber shop and asked him to go to Savannah to approve a barber chair Mr. Ford had picked out for him. The Emil J. Paider barber chair was 160 dollars and the plantation paid the bill. Mr. Ford also purchased a mirror, a cabinet, and two razors for the shop. In this photo, Mr. Carpenter is shown sitting in the chair Mr. Ford gave him. He is holding up the two razors Mr. Ford gave him. This photo was taken February 3, 1998, about sixty years after Mr. Ford gave him the chair and razors. He still uses them today and says the razors are just as sharp as they were the first time he used them. When Mr. Ford was at Richmond Hill, he visited the shop every other week. He continued the free rent and paid Carpenter three dollars for each haircut.

Mr. Ford passed away in 1947 and in 1951 the plantation was sold to International Paper Company. The local manager of the Paper Company told Carpenter he would have to buy the shop so he started paying 48 dollars per month until he got it paid for. He then moved the little wooden building to the backyard at his home. It is still there today and Carpenter still cuts hair part time. Customers sit in the same chair Mr. Ford gave him.

Mr. Carpenter is a significant part of Richmond Hill's history. When asked what kind of car he drives, Carpenter replied, "It's a Ford – I wouldn't drive anything else." Who could blame him?

CHERRY HILL SCHOOL

This photograph was taken prior to Mr. Ford building the George Washington Carver School. At that time there was no bus transportation to schools so consequently small one-room schools were located in each community to minimize walking distances. As soon as the George Washington Carver School was built these one-room schools were discontinued and the children were picked up in buses and taken to Carver. Mr. Ford had done some repair and painting on the one-room schools to improve them before Carver was built.

OAK LEVEL SCHOOL

This school was located in the Oak Level community about ten miles east of Richmond Hill. The children that had attended this school were transported by bus to the George Washington Carver School that was built by Mr. Ford. Some of the old desks out of this school are now on display at the Richmond Hill Historical Society Museum in the old Ford Kindergarten Building.

HENRY FORD AND
GEORGE WASHINGTON CARVER

George Washington Carver was a professor and botanist at Tuskeegee Institute in Tuskeegee, Alabama. He did a lot of work on the utilization of peanuts and sweet potatoes. Mr. Ford heard of his work and was interested in what he was doing. The Fords visited him in Tuskeegee. They decided to name the school for him and invited him to come to the dedication in March, 1940 while the Fords were in Richmond Hill.

GEORGE WASHINGTON CARVER SCHOOL

Mr. Ford built this school for the blacks in 1939 and the school was opened that year. The principal was Professor Herman Cooper. Mr. Ford had the children tested to find out the highest educational level. The highest level was fifth grade so the school started with six grade levels. Each year as students advanced another grade was added until there were eleven grades which was all the state schools had at that time. The school was modern in all respects with good equipment and furnishings. It was a very desirable place to teach. The teachers were provided with a teacherage next door in which to live. Their salaries were supplemented by Mr. Ford. Being so much better than most other black schools, they were able to attract very good teachers with a number of them having master's degrees.

GEORGE WASHINGTON CARVER TRADE SCHOOL

In addition to the classroom building, Carver had a Trade School where students were taught trades in wood and metal. The instructor was Charles Savage. Numerous metal and woodworking machines were in the shop to provide training for the students.

GEORGE WASHINGTON CARVER TEACHERAGE

The George Washington Carver teachers were provided a teacherage in which they could live. It was essentially identical to the Richmond Hill teacherage. They were operated slightly different. At George Washington Carver the teachers operated it themselves sharing expenses, whereas the Richmond Hill teachers paid a flat rate. The building was completely furnished and there was no charge for electricity nor for the use of the building. Essentially, they paid only for their food.

George Washington Carver Lunchroom

The George Washington Carver lunchroom was entirely financed by Mr. Ford. The meals were essentially the same as those served at the Richmond Hill lunchroom. In fact, the same person, Mrs. Pearl Carpenter, a Ford employee and the Richmond Hill lunchroom supervisor, worked out the menus for both. The Carver School had spacious grounds as can be seen.

George Washington Carver Chapel

The Bryan Neck Baptist Church, adjacent to the George Washington Carver School, was renovated by Mr. Ford to look very much like a Martha-Mary Chapel. It was used by the school as a chapel and by the community as a church. This was a rather unique utilization.

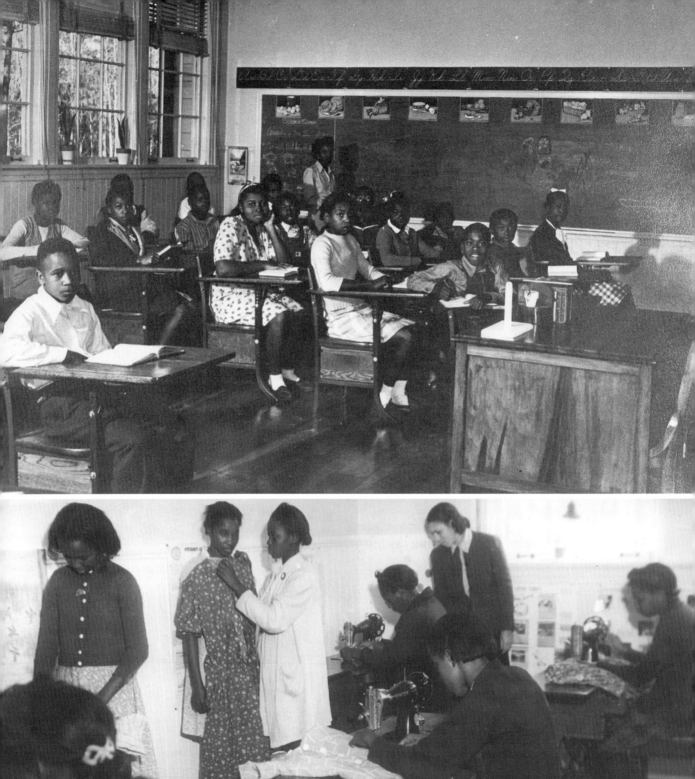

Typical George Washington Carver Classroom

A ll the classrooms were very nice. Note the large chalkboard and the natural light from the windows. The classes were relatively small. They were provided with individual comfortable desks and a desk for the teachers.

Sewing Classroom at Carver School

T he home economics department was provided with all the equipment and supplies they needed. Here in this sewing room you will note several sewing machines being used at one time. Also note the instructors providing assistance in sewing and fitting the dresses.

INTERIOR OF CARVER TRADE SCHOOL
DRILL PRESS

The Trade School was located immediately back of the classroom building. Here a student, Charles Mims, is shown operating a drill press as part of his shop training. The boys had ninety minutes of shop training three days per week. Through the window in the background can be seen part of the classroom building.

INTERIOR OF CARVER TRADE SCHOOL

In addition to academic training, the Carver students received manual training. Woodworking was part of this training. Here, Albert Brown learns to use a table saw.

CONSTRUCTION TRAINING

C harles Savage was the trade school instructor seen here in the left center foreground in a white shirt. In addition to shop training he believed in giving students practical training in small house construction with the idea that when they were out of school they could build their own house or work as a carpenter.

CARVER SCHOOL BUS

Transportation to and from school was furnished by Mr. Ford. These were nice buses with leather seats. They were the latest models available at the time. Note that the students lined up to enter the bus. There is no scrambling or pushing for position. In general, the youngest went first.

CARVER STUDENTS

Here three of the students at George Washington Carver reluctantly pose on the playground for their photograph.

SHOBIE FULTON

Shobie Fulton was the janitor at Carver School. He had worked at other jobs on the plantation but when Carver School was started he was selected to be the janitor. He was a very good, faithful, and reliable worker with a good personality. Everybody liked Shobie. I, personally, always enjoyed talking with him. He was somewhat of a comedian.

FIRST GRADE AT CARVER SCHOOL IN 1940

This picture of pupils in the first grade at Carver School was made on the front steps in 1940. A notation on the picture says first grade but I don't think they had such a large class under one teacher. It is possible that when the school first opened there may have been this many classified as first grade but had several teachers.

Reading From Left to Right
First Row Sitting:
James Harris
John Harris
Jerome Ferguson
Mamie Green
Delores Golden
Aldora Niles
Flora Cuthbert
Lilla Brown

Second Row:
Bennie Gray
Joseph Morrison
Christine Waldburg
Johnie Blake
Robert White
Joseph Bryant
James Hagro
Paul Blige
Robert Mitchell
Nathaniel Blige
Rosa Lee Thomas
Laura Blige
Rosa Anna Williams

Third Row;
William Jenkins
Henry Jordan
Edith Harris
Samuel Richardson
Eliza Blake
Emily Houston
Alphonso Golden
Willie Williams
Annie Johnson
Herman Niles
Elizabeth Blige
James Drayton
Willie Burke
Louise Lewis
Lucile Brown
Rosa Lee Perry

Fourth Row:
Mary Williams
Dorothy Smiley
Charles Barnard
Charles Perry
James Mitchell
Roland Mitchell
Willie Houston
Kermit Milton
Doretha Burg
Francena Mitchell
Hattie Niles
Josephine Houston
Charles Johnson

Fifth Row:
Harry Solomon
Paul Blige
Peter Blige
Cecile Blige
Samuel Halstion
Otis Devillars
Samuel Blige
Tena Brown
Willie Mae Houston
Marie Brown
Mary Blake
Gladys Solomon

Sixth Row:
Miss A.V. Haven
    Instructor of the first grade
Mr. Henry Ford
Mr. H.G. Cooper,
    Principal
Mr. Frank Campsall,
    Secretary to Mr. Ford
Mr. C.W. Savage,
    Trade School Instructor
Mr. J.F. Gregory
    Superintendent of Richmond
    Hill Plantation

FOURTH AND FIFTH GRADES AT CARVER SCHOOL IN 1940

This photograph of the fourth and fifth grade pupils at Carver in 1940 was made on the front steps of the school. Miss Sadye Westbrooks was the instructor.

Fourth and Fifth Grades
Reading From Left to Right;

First Row:
Charles Adams
Daniel Giles
Dan Brown
Abraham Blige
Margaret Alexander
Essie Morrison
Rudolph Harris
Susie Mae Mitchell
William Blige
Rufus Giles

Second Row:
Thomas Burke
Bennie Campbell
Benjamin Boles
Lena White
Nancy Morrison
Alice Bess
Elise Koger
Clifton Thomas
Thomas Green
Lucile Blige

Third Row:
Miss Sadye Westbrooks,
    Instructor
Gladys Blake
Horace Blige
Hattie Mae Jemison
Thomas Louis Jenkins
James Houston
Charles Boles Jr.
Ernest Loadholt

SUPERINTENDENT'S RESIDENCE

This was one of the first houses built on the plantation for employees, having been built in 1930 for Mr. Jack Gregory who at that time was superintendent of Ford Farms (later known as Richmond Hill Plantation). Mr. Gregory was superintendent from about 1930 until April of 1946. After that Mr. Ray Newman was superintendent.

The "Bottom" Village

This was the first housing project built by Mr. Ford for employees. It was called the "Bottom." The name came from the fact that the area had been a swamp or "bottom" before Mr. Ford had it cleared and drained. There were about seventy-five houses in this project. In the center of the project there was a block set aside for recreation. A baseball field was constructed on this area.

Some of the houses had two bedrooms but most had three. Each house had a building in back for an automobile, a laundry room, and a place to store firewood. Also in back was a space for a small garden. These houses were heated by a wood burning heater. The firewood usually came from the sawmill and delivered to the house for five dollars for a truck load. Note the neat driveways and the ditches to take care of drainage. Each driveway had a culvert which was bricked in on both sides. These houses were welcomed and appreciated by the employees and were occupied as soon as they were completed. Many of the employees who lived outside Richmond Hill were glad to get these houses so they could be nearer their work and to reduce travel cost.

No rent was charged employees until about 1945 when the Internal Revenue Service required that they be charged rent. Mr. Ford then made a charge of fifteen dollars a month for rent. He, in turn, then raised their pay fifteen dollars per month to take care of the rent.

Blueberry Village

The Blueberry Village was the second housing project Mr. Ford built. There were about sixty houses and they were about the same size as those in the "Bottom" Village. The "Bottom" Village was located in the eastern part of Richmond Hill and the Blueberry Village in the western part. These houses, like those in the "Bottom," were occupied as soon as completed. Like the other housing project, no rent was charged until 1945 and then only fifteen dollars per month.

FORD RESEARCH LABORATORY

A s you can see, this is not an impressive building. In fact, it is a very ordinary building. However, I can assure you that inside the building there was some very sophisticated and technical equipment for conducting research. Inside those walls, research was conducted on the conversion of farm products into products usable in the automotive industry. For example, rayon was made from local sweetgum and blackgum trees with the possibility for use as tire cord. Lignin plastics were made from corn cobs and sawdust suitable for gear shift knobs, distributor caps, and other small parts.

A soil testing laboratory was maintained to provide technical information on plantation soils relative to lime and fertilizer needs in the farming operations. Personnel in the laboratory included: Mr. Harry Ukkelberg, director, Mr. Frank McCall, chemist, Mr. Jack Oliver, chemist, and Leslie Long, technician, plus the necessary helpers. Additional help was hired during the summer.

I came to Richmond Hill in 1938 and was given a job in the research laboratory. I had just finished high school the year before and was working on our family farm and did not have a college degree at that time.

F. Leslie Long

Harry Gilbert Ukkelberg

Mr. Ukkelberg is shown here in the Ford Research Laboratory at Richmond Hill. He was director of the laboratory and in charge of all experimental work. He had been at the Thomas A. Edison Botanical Research Corporation in Ft. Myers, Florida conducting research on goldenrod and other rubber-producing plants. The laboratory at Ft. Myers had been financed by Henry Ford, Harvey Firestone, and Thomas A. Edison.

Mr. Edison passed away in 1931 and they needed someone to continue his work. Mr. Ukkelberg had done his graduate work at the University of Minnesota under Dr. Stakman and he recommended Mr. Ukkelberg for the job. Mr. Ukkelberg knew Mr. Firestone since he was in school with Firestone's son at the University of Minnesota. In fact, I think they roomed together for a time. Mr. Ford had a home across the street from the Edison Laboratory and visited once or twice a year. Mr. Ukkelberg met Mr. Ford at the laboratory. At that time, Mr. Ford had bought the property at Richmond Hill and was building his home here and was also building the research laboratory and needed someone to head up the research. Mr. Ukkelberg was chosen for the job and came to Richmond Hill in July 1936.

INSIDE THE RESEARCH LABORATORY

I was working in the laboratory and recall very well this photograph being taken. I had been operating the equipment in the left background determining the oil content of soybeans. The photo was taken by Mr. Bruce Riner who worked in the plantation office. On the left is Mr. Harry Ukkelberg, Laboratory Director. On the right is Mr. Jack Gregory, superintendent of the Plantation and in the center is Mr. Ford. Mr. Ukkelberg is holding a corn cob and Mr. Ford is holding a piece of plastic made in the laboratory from corn cobs. Mr. Ford had envisioned using plastics for automotive parts made from farm products. Mr. Ford said that the farmers were some of his best customers buying his cars, trucks, and tractors and he would like to buy their products and utilize them in the manufacturing of his automotive products. This photo was taken about 1940. Mr. Ford was way ahead of his time in his search for plastics for automobile parts. It is only in the last decade that plastics have become a significant part of automobiles.

RESEARCH LABORATORY SAMPLES

T he objective of the research laboratory was to conduct research on the conversion of farm products into products useable in the automotive industry. Mr. Ford always said the farmers were some of his best customers buying his cars, trucks, and tractors. In return, he would like to buy their products and covert them into products in auto making.

The samples shown in this photo are some of the better known of the farm-converted products. Mr. Ford, at one time, manufactured tires and was interested in rayon for tire cord. He had the forester make a survey of the timber on the plantation to find out how much there was of the different kinds. The survey showed there was more hardwood on the plantation than there was pine. Pine already had an established use for lumber, for making turpentine, and for making paper, so Mr. Ford wanted to use the hardwoods since they did not already have an extensive use like pine. Of the hardwoods, sweet gum and black gum was the most promising for making rayon.

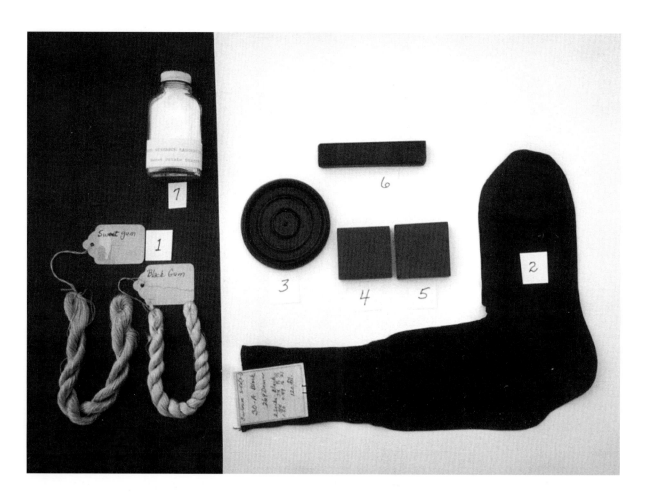

Mr. Ford hired two chemists from Savannah. They were Frank McCall and Jack Oliver. Mr. McCall had worked for the Herty Foundation Laboratory in Savannah and had conducted research on paper and rayon from pine. Mr. Oliver was a recent graduate form Clemson University in South Carolina. These two men were primarily responsible for the rayon and plastics research.

Sample no. 1 shows rayon samples. The one on the left is made from a sweet gum tree and the one on the right from a black gum tree. Although not made into tire cord, this is the basic rayon from which tire cord could be made. It was decided to make Mr. Ford a pair of socks from some of the rayon. Sample no. 2 shows one of these socks. The top, heel and toe are of cotton and remainder is rayon. When Mr. Ford was given these socks, he proudly wore them around the plantation. I don't think I have ever seen a man more proud of an accomplishment then he was of those socks. He would pull up his pants leg and show the socks saying, "See that – that used to be a sweet gum tree." Mr. McCall and Mr. Oliver deserve a great deal of credit for their fine research work.

Sample no. 3 is plastic made from corncobs. Some were also made from sawdust. It was molded in the form of a coaster but that was for testing purposes. This type of plastic was suitable for gear shift knobs and distributor caps. Sample no. 4 is also made from corncobs but in the form of tile. It was intended to replace ceramic tile in some cases. The basic product for moulding could be produced, at that time, for about four cents per pound and, thus, the finished product would be considerably cheaper than ceramic tile. The basic material in sample no. 5 is also made from corncobs but has a thin surface coat of red plastic to show that although the basic material was black, colors would also be available.

Sample no. 6 is a plastic that has been impregnated with ramie fiber prior to molding. Ramie fiber is a bast fiber that is extremely strong. It has been reported to have more tensile strength than steel, certainly on a weight basis. We had experimental plantings of ramie on the plantation. The ramie fiber added a great deal of strength to the plastic and could be grown successfully on the farm.

Sample no. 7 is sweet potato starch. Sweet potatoes were grown on the plantation for sale. Usually in growing sweet potatoes there are some that are too large to market called "jumbos". These are discarded or fed to hogs. When Mr. Ford found that we were throwing them away, he asked why we couldn't find a use for them. So we started looking into that. We first extracted the starch from these large sweet potatoes. It extracted very nicely and without any major purification problems. We examined the starch under the microscope and the starch grains looked a little different from other starch grains. Under the microscope they appeared as small white potatoes. We decided to send samples of this starch to companies manufacturing cloth and paper that use starch in sizing. They normally used corn starch for sizing but found that sweet potato starch went twice as far as corn starch. Thus, they could use half as much sweet potato starch as corn starch and get the same result. The companies were interested in the product and a plant was set up in Louisiana to produce sweet potato starch. It operated for a while but I don't know what happened to it. I think the companies started using a synthetic material.

After extracting the starch from the sweet potatoes in the laboratory, the major part of the sweet potato was left. This part we dried and ground finely to make a flour. Some of the flour was sent to the Community House where biscuits and rolls were made from it. These were distributed around the plantation for taste tests. Most agreed they were very good but no further tests were made.

JACK F. GREGORY

Mr. Jack Gregory, Superintendent of the Plantation, looks over some of the young lettuce in the Cherry Hill marsh field. This field was used for growing rice prior to the Civil War. Mr. Ford had it reclaimed and treated to make it suitable for growing lettuce and other field crops. The plantation usually grew 120-145 acres of lettuce each year. Some lettuce was grown on the Richmond marsh field but the soil tilth there was not nearly as good as the Cherry Hill marsh field, therefore, most of the lettuce was grown in the Cherry Hill field.

LETTUCE FIELD

This lettuce was reaching maturity and some of it nearly ready for harvest. In the center background can be seen a small building and a windmill. These were a significant part of growing lettuce in a reclaimed rice field. At times the rainfall exceeded the need of the lettuce and the excess needed to be drained off. When the tidal water in the river was higher than the field the water had to be pumped out. The windmill, with the connected pump, pumped the water into the river. When there was more water than the windmill could pump or when there was insufficient wind to operate it, an auxiliary pump was available. In the small building were two Ford V-8 motors powering a large auger-type water pump which had a large capacity. Incidentally, the pump was built in the Industrial Arts and Trade School. When operated at maximum capacity, it could pump 20,000 gallons of water per minute over the dike into the river. This high capacity was extremely important during heavy rains such as occur during a hurricane. The field was 300 acres and even an inch of rain would put over eight million gallons of water on the field.

THINNING LETTUCE

Lettuce was planted on bedded rows. When sufficient height was reached the plants were thinned to one plant per each eight to ten inches. These women were thinning the plants using hoes. Growing lettuce was a labor intensive operation.

HARVESTING LETTUCE

The lettuce was harvested by using a knife to cut beneath the head releasing it from the root system. The heads were then placed on a cart drawn by a tractor. The large cart had six smaller carts within it. All lettuce heads did not mature at the same time but over a period of several weeks. Therefore, several harvests had to be made over the same area. Bennie Sikes (far right) supervised the harvest.

Unloading Lettuce

At the packing shed the lettuce was unloaded from the carts into the shed. Unloading was made easier due to the smaller carts with caster wheels within the larger cart. The smaller carts could be rolled over to where the lettuce was trimmed and packed. The lettuce was packed in crates in three layers. The larger heads were packed 4 x 4 x 3 layers giving four dozen heads. The medium-sized heads were packed 4 x 5 x 3 layers giving five dozen heads. The smaller heads were packed 5 x 5 x 3 layers giving six dozen heads with three extras. Ice was placed in the crate with the lettuce, and after packing, the crates were placed in cold storage until picked up by a refrigerated truck. I have seen as much as eighteen tons loaded on one refrigerated tractor-trailer. Most of the lettuce produced was shipped to markets up and down the east coast.

Lettuce Packing Shed

Lettuce packing was an efficient operation. Even though a considerable amount of hand labor was necessary, part of the operation was mechanized. The lettuce trimmings were carried away by a conveyor. After being trimmed, the lettuce was placed on a conveyor belt which carried it through water washing and on to the packer. Each packer's stand had a box of ice easily accessible for placing ice between each layer of lettuce. When a crate was packed it was placed on a conveyor (see photo) which conveyed it (right to left in photo) to the place where ice was placed on top. A lid was then pressed down on top of the lettuce and nailed down by a person called a "nailer" while the press held it down. The nailer used a nail stripper and could press the top and nail it in about 15 seconds. The crate was then placed on a conveyor which carried it into the cold storage facility from which tractor trailers picked it up to take it to markets.

RICHMOND HILL
BRAND
ICEBERG
LETTUCE
GROWN AND PACKED BY
RICHMOND HILL PLANTATION, Inc.
RICHMOND HILL, GEORGIA
PRODUCE OF U.S.A.

LETTUCE LABEL

As you may know, all food products sold must be labeled as to what it is and who produced it. This is a copy of the label we placed on each crate of lettuce we sold. We usually planted from 120 to 145 acres of lettuce each year. It was grown in the areas that were once the rice fields prior to the Civil War. When Mr. Ford bought the property in 1925, the fields had long since grown up in trees and brush. The area was cleared, dikes restored, and drainage canals and ditches cleaned out to be functional again.

The soil had to be treated and modified to make it suitable for growing lettuce and other vegetables. The soil in each small area was sampled. All the soil testing was done in the research laboratory. The soil was treated according to the needs indicated by the soil tests. The lettuce we grew was Iceberg lettuce, a superior type of lettuce that is very tender and tasty. The lettuce grown on these brackish marsh soils was especially good, apparently due to the nature of these soils. Customers often told us it was pre-salted. The lettuce was so good that when we were packing lettuce the workers sometimes took along a jar of mayonnaise and ate a head at lunch time.

The house shown on the label is not the Ford residence but is symbolic of the plantation homes in the area prior to the Civil War. The lettuce was sold through a wholesale produce company in Savannah. Trucks picked it up at the lettuce packing shed. Most of these were very large tractor trailer rigs as they were called. I, personally, helped load 17 tons of lettuce on one tractor-trailer. The lettuce was sold mostly up the east coast. There was never a time that we were not able to sell all the lettuce we produced and we grew it for ten years.

PLANTATION ICE PLANT

A large amount of ice was necessary for the packing of the lettuce crop. At first the plantation purchased ice from the Savannah ice plants. However, this supply was gradually being depleted due to the increasing demand by nearby Fort Stewart, a military installation. When the lettuce packing operation was underway the plantation could not tolerate running out of ice. After all, lettuce was a perishable crop and must be immediately packed and shipped. Mr. Ford was not one to be dependent upon others and the plantation was already self-sufficient in many ways, so Mr. Ford built his own ice plant. It had a capacity of twelve tons per day which supplied all the ice needed for lettuce packing and some for other crops as needed. The excess ice was sold to other ice plants.

INTERIOR OF THE ICE PLANT

The ice was made in three hundred pound blocks in a metal container as shown here. These containers were hoisted and lowered into tap water to loosen the ice from the metal. After the ice was loosened from the metal container, it was released into the storage room. The workman shown here is Dick Crowley. This operation made possible a plentiful supply of ice for lettuce packing and other uses as well as sales to nearby companies in Savannah and to Fort Stewart.

BAILING RICE STRAW

Rice was grown on some of the marsh fields during the Ford Era. When the rice was threshed a large amount of straw was accumulated. Here the straw was being baled so that it could be sold or used for various purposes around the plantation. The rice produced on the plantation was processed through all the steps except it was not polished. Polishing rice removes the last very small amount of husk remaining on the grain. Unpolished rice has a much superior taste compared to polished rice. The very small amount of husk remaining on the grain gives it a very distinctive taste. No wonder so much rice was consumed in a coastal area where it was grown. Today all rice for sale in the grocery stores is polished. The unpolished rice produced on the plantation was packaged in bags of various sizes and sold in the commissary. Some was sold in fifty pound bags. Rice keeps well so some people would buy enough to last until the next year's harvest.

Blacksmith Shop

Some of the repairs made around the plantation which required blacksmithing were done in this shop. It was sometimes necessary to fabricate parts for the farm machinery and for the sawmill. Here Richard Smith is shown operating a drill press.

VALAMBROSIA PLANTATION HOUSE

Little is known about the Valambrosia Plantation. It was located in Chatham County across the Ogeechee River from Mr. and Mrs. Ford's residence and bought to assure their privacy. The Fords purchased the property in the early 1930's. It too had been a rice plantation with a large acreage of marshland planted to rice along the Ogeechee River. Mr. Ford had the large plantation home restored as shown here.

VALAMBROSIA FIELD

The Valambrosia farm was in the adjoining county of Chatham and across the river from the Ford residence. There were numerous jobs to be done around the plantation. One such job was pruning the pecan trees. This workman is hauling off the pruned limbs. I know the reader is not surprised to see he is driving a Ford tractor. He is also hauling with a wagon made from a Ford chassis.

VALAMBROSIA CABBAGE

This workman shows off some of the cabbage produced on the Valambrosia farm. This farm consisted of about 4300 acres but not much of it was cleared for field crops. However, numerous vegetable crops were grown on the cultivated areas. The vegetables were usually sold in Savannah.

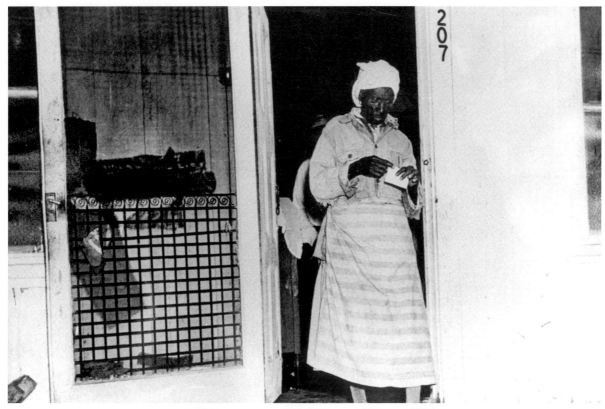

Valambrosia Apartment

Mr. Ford bought property across the Ogeechee River from his residence in Chatham County. It was called Valambrosia Plantation. Before the Civil War it had been a rice plantation. Mr. Ford farmed the area and built apartments for some of the help. These were very nice and convenient small apartments.

Peter Warner

Some of the farm work at Valambrosia was done using mules. Peter Warner was responsible for taking care of the mules. He was a good, honest, and faithful worker. He is living today and must be at least 100 years old.

TRIMMING A SAW LOG

Furnishing the sawmill with enough logs to keep it running steadily was no easy task, particularly if it was running at its capacity of about 90,000 board feet per day. Here a workman trims the limbs from a felled tree which is one of the first things to be done.

DRAGGING A LOG

After the log was trimmed it was dragged to a central location where it could be loaded on the log truck. Today there is more modern and efficient machinery for moving logs in the woods. Mr. Ford was really more interested in giving people a job than in efficiency here.

LOADING LOGS

A fter the logs were dragged to a central location, they were loaded onto the log truck using a dragline as shown in this picture and hauled to the sawmill.

SAWMILL

The sawmill was a very large one. This photo shows only a portion of it. In addition to two large steam boilers in the sawmill building, there were two more in the powerhouse building to the right and out of view in this photo. The powerhouse boilers also furnished steam to operate a steam engine which pulled a direct current generator to furnish electricity to the Industrial Arts and Trade School. Most of the motors powering the machines in the trade school were D.C. motors. The two boilers in the sawmill burned sawdust and the two boilers in the powerhouse burned shavings from the planing mill. Beyond the sawmill to the rear were the planing mill, cabinet shop, and other accessory sections. To the left out of view was the lumber yard and the dry kiln. The lumber yard covered more than an acre where lumber held in reserve was stacked. There were rail tracks from the sawmill to and throughout the lumber yard where loaded carts could be rolled to the stacks. There were also rail tracks to the dry kiln. There was a very interesting aspect to the sawmill operation. Mr. Ford had employed a full-time forester. He had the forester make a survey to find out how many board feet of timber was growing on the plantation each day. It turned out to be 15,000 board feet and that is all Mr. Ford would let them saw per day. He said in that way the sawmill could operate indefinitely. However, when World War II came along, there was a great demand for lumber in the shipyards in Savannah and by Fort Stewart, so he allowed them to saw to capacity which was about 90,000 board feet per day.

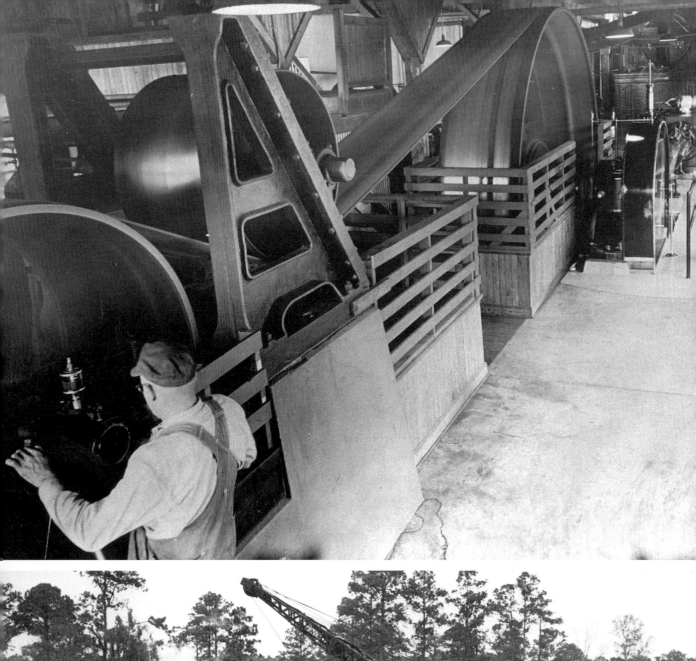

SAWMILL STEAM ENGINE

An indication of the size of the engine which pulled the sawmill can be noted from this photograph. The man in the left foreground is Ollie Judy. In the far right background is Leslie Cribbs. Both of these gentlemen lived in Ford built houses. In front of Cribbs is the large power wheel of the engine. Note that he is standing about the center of the wheel and that part of wheel is below ground level and the upper portion of the wheel is several feet above his head. The wheel appears to be at least 14 feet in diameter which is a tremendously large wheel for a sawmill. The engine was so powerful that when the full load of the sawmill was placed on it there was no detectable change in speed.

LOGS AT SAWMILL

When logs were brought into the sawmill they were separated according to species, quality and size using a dragline as shown here. One man operated the dragline and another "dogged" and "undogged" the logs. The separation increased the sawing efficiency in the sawmill particularly when orders were for certain sizes and lengths of lumber.

Elevating Logs

A t the sawmill logs were elevated to the second floor for sawing. In the right background there is a trough in the bottom of which there is a moving steel chain with cleats on it. When the log is rolled into the trough it is elevated to the second floor. The logs are rolled down the ramp (log brow) on the left, one at a time into the trough. Note the arch over the log as it proceeds up the trough. It has a semicircle of water being sprayed on the logs to remove soil and sand from the logs to prevent dulling the saw.

Saw Filing

S aw filing was an essential part of the sawmill operation. It was necessary to keep plenty of saws on hand and to have them sharp. A sharp saw must be ready when needed so that it could be installed immediately to minimize down time. There was a special filing room.

SAWING AREA

In the center of the photograph behind the circle saw is Judson Anderson, sawyer, and on the carriage are Abraham Demere and Irwin Brown. The two workers on the left are unknown. To the right of the saw is the carriage on which Demere and Brown are riding and which pulls the log into the saw. In this photograph the log has already been squared up. In the sequence of the sawing, the carriage is run back toward the rear of the building where a log is rolled onto the carriage. As soon as it is on the carriage it is clamped down in place by steam operated "dog." The carriage then moves the log to the saw where a slab is sawed off the side. When the carriage goes back, the log is flipped 90 degrees so that the flat side is now on bottom. The carriage comes back and the saw takes off another slab. The procedure is repeated until the removal of the slabs has squared up the log. After that, the log can be sawed into whatever size of lumber is needed within the limits of the square. The carriage is pulled along by cables that wrap around a drum which is powered. After a slab or board has been sawed off and the carriage returned back beyond the saw, a workman on the carriage pulls a lever which moves the log over into the saw for the next cut.

TRANSPORTING LUMBER

The sawed lumber that is to go to the planing mill, the dry kiln, or the lumber yard is moved by means of a rail cart having steel wheels running on a steel rail. Thus heavy loads could be moved with a minimum of effort.

Planing Mill

Sawed lumber that is to be planed is directed to the planing mill. Here a workman feeds the lumber into the planing machine. After being planed the lumber is stored in a dry place.

TRUCKING LUMBER

Lumber that is to be used on the plantation is placed on trucks and taken to the site. For example, if the carpenters are building a house on the plantation, the construction foreman would place an order to the sawmill for certain lumber to be delivered to a certain job site at a certain time. Sawmill workers would load it on trucks to deliver to the site.

SHIPPING LUMBER VIA RAILROAD

Some of the lumber produced at the sawmill was sold and shipped by rail on the Seaboard Airline Railway which ran through Richmond Hill. This was particularly true during World War II. Part of the sawmill can be seen in the left background.

CHIPPING A "STREAK" ON PINE TREE

Mr. Ford maintained a turpentine operation on the plantation. He apparently did this to give jobs to those workers whose trade was turpentine. Ben Smith is shown putting a "streak" on a pine tree cutting through the bark and cambium layer to release the gum (sap) which runs down into the cup. The tool he is using is called a "hack". The "hack" has a handle about 14 inches long and 2-3 inches in diameter. To the top of the handle a "U" shaped blade is attached and to the bottom a weight to aid in cutting the "streak". A "streak" is put on once a week and after four or five weeks the gum is harvested from the cup. It takes a great deal of skill and experience to be able to use this tool properly. The tool must be kept very sharp. The cut must be straight and the correct vertical height of about one-eighth inch. Note that an empty cup is placed over the cup receiving the gum. This is done to prevent the wood chips from entering the gum cup. An alternative to this, often used, was to use a paddle with a handle and place it over the cup while chipping.

TYPICAL TURPENTINE WOODS

These pine trees have been worked to a height of about six feet. When the trees have been worked up to about three or four feet, the cup at the bottom is moved to a higher level on the tree as seen in this photograph. A "hack" is used to put a "streak" on the trees until it is worked up to a height that is uncomfortable for using a "hack" and then a "puller" is used. The streak on these trees would have been put on with a "puller." Mr. Ford had this kind of fence put along this road. The site is about ten miles east of Richmond Hill on the west side of the Belfast road.

TURPENTINE WOODS

Ben Smith secures a pine from fire. In the turpentine business it is a common practice to burn off the woods in winter to keep down the underbrush to make the trees more accessible. Since turpentine gum (sap) is flammable, it is necessary to shield the tree from fire during the burn off. This is done by hoeing around the tree so that there is no flammable material leading up to the tree.

Dipping Gum

When the cup on the tree has sufficient gum in it, the gum is put (dipped) into a hand-carried bucket of about five gallon size. After going to numerous trees and collecting sufficient gum to fill the bucket it is carried to a barrel and emptied.

EMPTYING GUM INTO BARREL

This photograph shows gum from the bucket being emptied into a barrel of about fifty gallons capacity. The full barrel is picked up by a wagon or truck. There is a screw-on lid called a "head" that is placed on the barrel so that it can be turned down and rolled. The barrel is then elevated into the wagon or truck by rolling the barrel up "skids" which are usually poles about four inches in diameter and about twenty feet long. The barrel and the gum weighs about six hundred pounds and it takes a strong man to roll it up. Two men are used where possible.

OLD TURPENTINE STILL

This turpentine still was on the premises when Mr. Ford bought the property. This photograph is a relatively closeup view of the still and is included here in order that the process of distillation can be, at least, partially explained. To the left is the platform where the gum is delivered by wagons or trucks. From the platform the barrels of gum are rolled up the ramp to the upstairs of the still. There it is emptied into the still. The still size varies but the most common size was five 50-gallon barrels. The still tank is solid copper. A large copper cap is placed on the neck of the still and connected to the cap is a large copper pipe which enters a very large diameter tank of cool water. When the fire is started under the still and the vapor starts coming off it goes through the copper pipe and through the cool water where the vapor is condensed to gum spirits of turpentine. The process is continued until essentially all of the spirits of turpentine has been distilled from the gum. After the major portion of the spirits has been distilled, a small amount of water is continually added which assists in the distillation of the remaining spirits. The time required for distillation of a "charge" varies depending on several factors but generally takes about three hours. What remains in the tank is turpentine rosin and is extremely hot but must be removed from the tank while very hot because it solidifies upon cooling. The wood fire is removed from the furnace under the still. The cap is removed and using a large strainer with a long wooden handle most of the chips that entered the still with the gum are removed from the hot rosin. The hot rosin is then run out into a vat below. Before this can happen, a great deal of preparation is required. The hot rosin must be filtered and the filtration equipment must be placed over the vat. It consists of two large screens as large as the vat. The top screen contains a one-sixteenth inch mesh wire screen supported by a one-fourth inch mesh hardware cloth. The second screen below is a cotton pad supported by a screen and hardware cloth. After the screen and cotton filter are all in place, a trough is placed between the screen and the valve on the still. All this preparation is done while the gum is distilling so it will be ready when the rosin is ready to be released. When the valve is opened and the rosin is released, it flows through the trough onto the screens and filters and into the vat. While the rosin is in the vat it must be stirred frequently to prevent it from becoming semi-solid in the bottom. After the rosin has been released from the distillation tank, some water must be poured into the copper tank to prevent it from getting too hot even though the fire has been removed. If it got too hot it would warp. After sufficient cooling, the rosin is dipped up into rosin barrels. These are barrels made of wood staves and includes a top and bottom. They are put together at the still and it takes a great deal of skill and experience to do it. The top does not have to be liquid rosin tight since it is not put on until the rosin has cooled and solidified. The bottom of the barrels are caulked with stiff clay in case there is a small crack where the rosin might leak out. The gum spirits of turpentine which

was distilled off is placed in a very tight commercially made wooden barrel made of oak. The barrel is sealed internally with a glue at the still and allowed to dry prior to placing turpentine in it. The yield of turpentine and rosin varies according to the type of gum being distilled. A typical yield from five fifty-gallon barrels of gum would be fifty gallons of turpentine and three and one-fourth barrels of rosin. The rosin barrels are slightly less than fifty-gallon capacity. There is much more to the distillation process than can be described here but hopefully this will be enough to give the reader a general understanding of what the distillation process involves. From this description one can easily see that the turpentine workers who worked for the plantation stayed busy and had to be skilled.

FORD TURPENTINE STILL

Mr. Ford had this still built about 1938 in a pine forest about ten miles east of Richmond Hill on what was called the Belfast Siding road. No one seems to know why he had it built. Although there was some income to be derived from the turpentine operation, I'm sure that was not his objective. My belief is that he did it to employ those people who had worked in turpentine and that was the trade they knew and they needed employment after Mr. Ford bought the property.

OYSTER SHUCKING HOUSE

Mr. Ford seemed to be interested in any enterprise along the coast in which people made a living. Mr. Ford was even interested in oystering. Heretofore, people gathered oysters from the river, took them home, shucked and sold them. Here on the Kilkenny River, Mr. Ford built an oyster shucking house. Most of the oyster harvesting was done in the winter. Note the smokestack indicating that heat was provided inside for the workers. The oysters were harvested using boats and were brought inside this building where they were shucked.

This was not a large operation but was limited to available oysters. Mr. Ford realized these limits and planted oysters. This was done by placing cypress shingles in the marsh along the river. They had to be placed at a specific level relative to the tide. The oysters would grow on the shingles.

The shucked oysters were sold in the Ford Commissary at very reasonable prices. Employees and others were able to buy fresh oysters at any time during the oyster season. These oysters were the freshest possible, being brought directly from the river, shucked and brought straight to the Commissary. It almost seems impossible that Mr. Ford would be interested in a small project like this, but he certainly was.

SHUCKING OYSTERS

For the purposes of the camera, this lady is shown outside shucking an oyster. To shuck an oyster, one uses an oyster knife. This is not an ordinary knife as it does not have a sharp blade. It is a double-edged blade used to pry open the oysters. It takes a great deal of experience to become proficient in shucking oysters. The shucker wears a thick glove on the hand holding the oyster because the edges of the oyster are thin and sharp and would cut your hand without protection.

KILKENNY HOUSE

M r. Ford purchased this property on June 27, 1930. It had changed ownership may times. It was originally granted by the King of England to Thomas Young on June 29, 1766, and was composed of 1000 acres. From time to time, Thomas Young acquired various tracts of land previously granted to Jacob Lockerman, Nathaniel Yates, Morgan Sabb, George Cubbedge, and Sir Edward Powell. On January 21, 1836, executors of Thomas Young conveyed to Charles W. Rogers 4,570 acres known as Kilkenny and Belvedere. Then in that same year on December 14, 1836, it was conveyed to Charles W. Rogers, Jr. By will probated on May 15, 1861, it went to Charles Rogers. Presumably, he was the son of Charles W. Rogers, Jr. By will of C.W. Rogers dated February 19, 1863, the property was given to his sister, Anna W. West, the wife of Dr. J.J. West. This included Kilkenny and Lincoln Plantations. On November 23, 1874, it was conveyed to James M. Butler. From Butler, on January 15, 1890, it was conveyed to James M. Furber. From Furber, on February 6, 1900, it was conveyed to William L. Nevin. From Nevin on February 13, 1901, it was conveyed to Kilkenny Plantation, a corporation. Then on March 27, 1918, it was conveyed to Kilkenny Land and Cattle Company. On February 4, 1926, it was conveyed to Kilkenny Land Corporation. Then on June 27, 1930, it was conveyed to Henry Ford. Some of the above information was obtained from the records of Henry Ford Museum and Greenfield Village Research Center.

When Mr. Ford bought the property, the house was in a rundown condition. The house had been built in 1843-46 by Charles W. Rogers, Jr. Mr. Rogers named the plantation Kilkenny in honor of Kilkenny Castle in Ireland. In his home at that time could be found several paintings of the Irish castle. The paintings disappeared during the transition from one owner to another.

Although Kilkenny house was rundown when Mr. Ford bought it, it had been remodeled several times and bore little resemblance to the original house that Mr. Rogers had built. Mr. Ford had it restored to its original grandeur. The house faced the Kilkenny River and was located only about 150 feet from it. At that time, all homes along the coast faced the rivers since there were few roads and the rivers were the primary means of transportation both for personal travel and obtaining supplies. During the Civil War, the house was fired upon by Union forces using cannons from ships located in the intracoastal waterway (in this case, Bear River). The barn was hit by one cannon and the house by two. When Mr. Ford started restoring the house, the carpenters found where the cannon ball had severed one of the uprights in the front wall. It was shown to Mr. Ford and he would not let them replace it. He said to frame it and put a small door there so people could open the door and see what had happened. It was fixed that way and is still there today.

Note some of the features of the house. The cupola on top of the house was used by family members to look out over the river toward the ocean to observe family members or friends who might be out there. In case trouble was visible, they could send help. Also note the small windows at the base of the top roof. These were just above the upstairs floor level. They were for ventilation. The summers were hot and the ventilation provided some ocean breezes. The two windows downstairs

on each side of the front door could be fully opened and provided a cooling breeze for downstairs.

In the far left background of the photograph can be seen part of a small building. This is the kitchen. During that time, kitchens were not part of the main house due to the fire hazard. The kitchen has a very large fireplace and a Dutch oven. The foods were cooked in iron pots which hung on an iron rod over the fire. The Dutch oven was to the side of the fireplace. The building has two rooms and a small attic room. The food was prepared in the room with the fireplace. On the other side was apparently where the servants ate. The attic room was probably used for sleeping by the cooks.

Mr. Ford also restored some of the slave cabins. They were very nice and photographs are shown below. Today the property is owned by Mr. Robert Bacot, Sr., who operates an adjoining marina.

KILKENNY COLONIAL KITCHEN

In those days it was the custom to have the kitchen separated from the house This was because of the fire hazard. There was no way to put out a fire except with a few buckets of water. Therefore, the kitchen was placed sufficiently far enough away from the house so that if it should catch fire the house could be saved.

This Colonial kitchen was restored by Mr. Ford and is still standing today in back of the Kilkenny plantation house. It is the property of Mr. Robert Bacot, Sr. As viewed in this photo, on the right side of the building is a very large fireplace with a steel rod extending over the fire area on which pots were hung for cooking. On one side of the fireplace is a Dutch oven for baking. On the left side of the building there is a table that apparently was used to prepare the food for cooking and for the cooks to eat. An attic room appears to have been used as sleeping quarters for cooks.

KILKENNY SLAVE CABINS

In addition to Mr. Ford restoring the Kilkenny house, he also restored some of the nearby slave cabins. This photo shows two that were restored. Note the neat appearance of the little cabins. Each had a chimney and fireplace for heating and cooking. They are no longer standing today. In those early days the cabins were painted with "whitewash", a mixture of water and lime. These were restored in the same way.

STRATHY HALL

S trathy Hall was built about 1840 but underwent several alterations and additions over the years before Mr. Ford bought it. This photo shows the library addition on the right side of the house and an upstairs room. There appears to be a two story addition on the left rear. When Mr. Ford bought the property he had all the additions removed and the house restored to its original state. A photo on page 266 shows it after restoration.

Strathy Hall Parlor

According to the best available records, this photograph was made about 1910. Even in those early days the interior was beautiful. Note the fireplaces and accessories. Notice the fringed trim around the mantel and the lace curtains.

Strathy Hall Dining Room

The dining room does not appear as fancy as the parlor. However, it is still nice for that time. Note the chair in the center background, the wallpaper, and the light over the table which appears to be Alladin or gas. The kitchen was separated from the main house out back.

STRATHY HALL LIBRARY

This is believed to be the library after Sherman's troops destroyed the books. Through a curtained doorway one views a room containing a writing desk and a wicker rocker with a footstool. The fireplace mantel has shelves with dishes and other objects displayed. Framed pictures are on the shelves. The walls are papered, the floor has carpet, and the ceiling and arched doorway are paneled. One of the books destroyed by the troops was an original Tyndale Bible.

STRATHY HALL TODAY

Capt. James Mackay was granted 100 acres on the site of Strathy Hall in 1755. He was granted additional acreage over a period of several years. It was named after the ancestral home of the Mackays in Scotland — Strathnaver. Capt. Mackay served with George Washington in the French and Indian War and also in the Revolution. After giving up his army commission he served on the council for the royal governors and remained loyal to Great Britain. He was held in high esteem by his contemporaries and was addressed as "The Honorable Capt. James Mackay, of Strathy Hall". In 1785, Capt. Mackay was ill and went by boat to Rhode Island in search of medical treatment. Returning by land, he died in Virginia. The Mackay mansion had been destroyed long ago. The only trace was the ancient live oaks which were probably there during Capt. Mackay's lifetime. In 1817 Strathy Hall was sold to George W. McAllister who later added to the 1420 acre tract by further purchases. At one time Strathy Hall was a rice plantation growing rice in the marsh land across the Ogeechee River from the house. One of McAllister's daughters, Matilda Willis, married Thomas Savage Clay. The property passed into the hands of their son, Robert Harbersham Clay, in 1878 and from him to his widow, Eva Millis Clay, who conveyed the property to Mr. Ford. The present Strathy Hall house appears much as it was when built in about 1840. It had been added onto several times over the years to accommodate the large family and family connections so that it was a large house when Mr. Ford acquired ownership. It had not been occupied by the Clays for a number of years and was deteriorating.

At the beginning of the Civil War it contained a large library in which there was an original Tyndale Bible. The library was ransacked and scattered over a square mile by Sherman's troops. The house was not burned because the soldiers did not want to alert Ft. McAllister that they were in the vicinity. However, the soldiers did use the house. When Ford restored Strathy Hall he had it returned to the original plain plantation style by removing all the various additions. This method of restoration resulted in its being placed on the National Register of Historic Places. His techniques were also copied in some Williamsburg restorations.

International Paper sold the property and it was bought by Neill and June Baylor who live there today. The Baylors have taken excellent care of the place as can be seen from this recent photograph.

COTTENHAM HOUSE

The Cottenham Plantation house was one of the most beautiful of all the plantation houses along the coastal rivers. It was not restored by Mr. Ford but he liked it so much that he patterned the Community House after it. I was told that Mr. Ford planned to tear it down and build the Community House from it, but as it turned out the Community House needed to be larger and so that was not done. However, I believe some of the larger timbers were used in the Community House. Also, the mantels in the ballroom may have come from Cottenham. The Cottenham House gradually deteriorated and today at the site there is no sign of it. It was located on Red Bird Creek south of Fort McAllister.

In Mr. Edward Cutler's reminiscences, at the Henry Ford Museum and Greenfield Village in Dearborn, Michigan, he said the Cottenham House still had beautiful furniture in it when he was down here but the wallpaper was hanging down from the ceiling almost to the floor. No one knows what happened to the furnishings. Mr. Cutler was here in 1936, overseeing the construction of the Ford residence.

WHITEHALL

Whitehall Plantation, comprising 2600 acres, was purchased August 22, 1925, by Mr. Ford from Mrs. Thomas Arnold (Elizabeth W. Arnold), Mary G.A. Nash, and Louisa G.A. Jackson. The Whitehall house had burned March 29, 1914. It had been unoccupied for a long time and had deteriorated so much that the porches had collapsed. The house caught fire from a woods fire.

The Whitehall property was originally granted to James Mackay who left it to his grandson, Stephen Maxwell, who sold it to Joseph Clay as trustee in a marriage settlement between Barbara Clark and Abraham Gindrat, whose daughter, Louisa, married Richard Arnold. Richard and Louisa Arnold were well known as the owners and operators of Whitehall. Richard was a very successful rice planter. It has been reported that in one year he produced one million pounds of rice. Richard Arnold was a businessman from Rhode Island. After his marriage to Louisa, the Arnolds spent the winters at Whitehall and the summers in Rhode Island. It was the custom of wealthy southern planters to spend summers up north and the winters down south on their plantations. Arnold organized and managed his land well and since he had income from northern businesses and wanted additional property he added to his original land holdings by purchasing Cherry Hill Plantation, Sans Souci, Sedgefield and Orange Grove. He also rented Mulberry. He had 11,000 acres of land before the Civil War. He grew rice, Sea Island cotton, and sugar cane for syrup and sugar. He constructed his own large brick sugarmill at Cherry Hill. He also had cattle and sheep and of course grew other crops to feed the slaves on his lands. He had docks and ships for shipping his products to market in Savannah.

The Arnold family was divided by the Civil War. Richard turned his plantations over to his sons, Thomas and William Elliott who were sympathetic to the Confederacy and who served in the army. Richard, Louisa and the other members of the family went to Rhode Island for the duration of the war. After the war Richard returned to Whitehall and again assumed ownership. The plantations had been severely damaged but with money from his northern businesses he restored them and became the largest rice producer in the state. Arnold died in 1873, leaving Cherry Hill to his son William Elliott and Whitehall to his son Thomas. William Elliot apparently was not a good manager and Cherry Hill was sold at a sheriff's sale. Thomas was like his father but died in 1875 and Whitehall was sold to settle the estates. Mrs. Thomas Arnold (Elizabeth W. Arnold) was living in Rhode Island when Mr. Ford bought the property from her and Mary G. A. Nash and Louisa G.A. Jackson. There is a letter in the Ford Archives of the Henry Ford Museum and Greenfield Village from Mrs. Arnold dated May 28, 1925 to Mr. Ford asking that the family cemetery at Whitehall be preserved. Today the property surrounding the cemetery is owned by Mr. and Mrs. Toby Roberts who are, thankfully, sympathetic to the preservation of the cemetery.

There were two other tracts associated with Whitehall which were purchased by Mr. Ford. The Harewood tract which adjoined Whitehall was conveyed to Mr. Ford by deed of March 31, 1925. Then there was an unnamed 275-acre tract conveyed to Mr. Ford by warranty deed of April 16, 1925.

WILL BROWN COTTAGE

When Mr. Ford bought the Richmond Hill property there was a small shack on the south-west corner of what is now Ford Avenue and Pine Crest Street near the railroad. It was occupied by Will Brown who was crippled in both legs and unable to work. Mr. Ford reconstructed the shack and made it a comfortable little cottage. Mr. Ford took care of Will Brown as long as he lived.

Aunt Jane Lewis

On the back of a photograph of Aunt Jane in the Ford Archives at the Henry Ford Museum and Greenfield Village in Mrs. Ford's handwriting is as follows: "Old Aunt Jane (slave woman) we found in Darien, Georgia, living on what she could beg. Mr. Ford and I built her a little house and cared for her until she passed away."

Nurse Reed from the Ford Clinic in Richmond Hill Plantation went to Darien to check on her once a week taking any medicine she needed. If the nurse thought necessary, Dr. Holton was sent from Savannah to check on her or she was carried to his office in Savannah. Another example of how the Fords helped people in the area.

AUNT JANE'S HOUSE

This is the little house that Mr. and Mrs. Ford built for Aunt Jane. Note that it is a nice neat little house built beside the old one she was living in. This is very characteristic of the way the Fords helped people in this area. After Mr. and Mrs. Ford passed away and the plantation was sold, Mr. Herman Cooper, former principal of George Washington Carver School, bought the house.

LONDON HARRIS COOKING CANE SYRUP

London Harris owned a small parcel of land near Richmond Hill. He did not sell it to Mr. Ford. In addition to other crops, he grew sugar cane. In the fall he harvested the cane, extracted the juice, and boiled (concentrated) it to make cane syrup. It was important as a food and as a sweetener for other foods in this part of the country for many years. Harris made syrup for his family and for sale.

LONNIE PATTERSON

Lonnie Patterson was a blacksmith in charge of the Blacksmith Shop. On Saturdays he operated a grist mill on Ford property. For the benefit of those not familiar with a grist mill, it is a mill used to grind corn into meal or grits. In those days it was common for farmers to take corn to the grist mill to be ground into meal or grits for their own use. This photo shows Patterson pouring corn into the mill. The mill was powered by a Fordson tractor.

LONNIE PATTERSON RESIDENCE

This house was on the Ford property and Lonnie Patterson lived there for many years while he worked for the Ford Plantation. The house is typical of many houses either owned or occupied by blacks at that time.

FORD GREENHOUSE

The greenhouse was adjacent to the Research Laboratory. It was used for research and for growing flowering plants for Mrs. Ford so that they would be ready when the Fords came down in January. It was heated with hot water from the wood-fired boiler. Pansies, violets, gladiola, King Alfred daffodils and jonquils were some of the flowers that must be in adequate supply for Mrs. Ford and in first quality condition. Some of these were also sent to the community house for use in arrangements there. It was important that a large number of violets in bloom be maintained as Mrs. Ford had borders of these in the residence garden. At night deer frequently ate them. An early rising gardener replaced the eaten ones with blooming plants before Mrs. Ford got up. These were a special variety of violets which Mrs. Ford had sent down from Dearborn.

Adjacent to the greenhouse an outdoor nursery of additional small plants and roses was also maintained as fresh cut flowers were used in the community house in arrangements at all times.

LUCY BUNCE

L ucy Bunce, one of the authors, looks over some of the pansies being grown in the greenhouse for Mrs. Ford.

I came to Richmond Hill in 1940 to teach science (chemistry, biology, physics) and mathematics (algebra, geometry, trigonometry) in the Richmond Hill High School. At that time the school enrollment was small and I taught all the science and mathematics classes in the school. During World War II, I served as clerk of the War Price and Rationing Board on which was Mr. Ukkelberg, chairman, Mr. Bascom Mahaffey, and Mr. Louis Gill. During the war, many service men's wives were available to teach and the men on the rationing board wanted me as their clerk. I taught again after the war was over. Later Mr. Newman, superintendent of the plantation, asked me to work as payroll clerk in the plantation office, which I did from 1949 until the plantation was sold to International Paper Company in November, 1951.

In the years I was teaching, I worked in the research laboratory during the summer. I became interested in the history and activities of the plantation and was frequently called upon to show visitors around the plantation. I even climbed to the "widow's walk" on the top of the Kilkenny House with them for the beautiful view of the Kilkenny river, marsh, and two barrier islands, Ossabaw and St. Catherines.

I also became interested in Leslie Long who worked in the research laboratory and we were married June 20, 1943, in the Martha-Mary Chapel and had our reception in the Community House.

Lucy Bunce Long

ROAD MAINTENANCE

During the Ford era at Richmond Hill, none of the roads east of Richmond Hill were paved. They were all dirt. Road maintenance men, who were Richmond Hill Plantation employees using plantation equipment shown here, maintained the dirt roads in the best possible condition, particularly when the Fords were here. Sometimes this was difficult to do after heavy rains.

BELFAST CLUB HOUSE

This house was built on the banks of the Belfast River for the employees to use as an outing. There was a sign-up sheet in the office where employees or employee social groups could reserve it for specific times.

On the left in this photo is an interesting structure which most readers may never have heard about. Yes, they know about the water tank but not about the force which put the water up there. No electricity or engine of any kind was used. It was a unique and ingenious device called a "ram". It is difficult to explain how it works without seeing it but I will try. It worked where there was a flowing well of sufficient size. For example, let's say it is a 4-inch diameter well that flows. As the water flowed up from the well it pushed a cap up where it tripped a valve which very suddenly stopped the water flow which created an instantaneously high water pressure which opened another small check valve to a smaller pipe. The sudden pressure in this smaller pipe forced a small percentage of the water up to the tank. It, of course, operated continuously and although the percentage of flowing water which was forced up into the tank was small, it was sufficient to keep the tank full of water unless large amounts of water were used. The tank had an overflow pipe so that when it was full, the excess water could drain away. I don't know who invented this device but it was a very clever one for areas where electricity was not available. They are not used today because the wells here do not flow anymore from the aquifer.

GORDON CARPENTER'S STORE

This old country store was at the community of Keller about ten miles east of Richmond Hill. Mr. Carpenter did not sell his property to Ford but continued to operate this little country store until his death. This store provided the shopping needs of the community for such staple items as sugar, flour, rice and even livestock medicines. Note the old type gasoline pump. The gas was pumped by hand up into a glass cylinder at the top. The cylinder held five gallons. A hose delivered the gas from the cylinder to the gas tank of the car by gravity. Electricity was not available in this area until the Rural Electrification Administration (R.E.A.) provided it.

No paved roads were in the area so that when it rained the roads would become very muddy as seen in this photograph.

KELLER KINDERGARTEN

Mr. and Mrs. Ford built this kindergarten at Keller, a community about ten miles east of Richmond Hill, before they built the one at Richmond Hill. This was probably built about 1937 or 1938. Note the playground equipment on the left. All this was free to any child wishing to attend.

KELLER KINDERGARTEN PLAYGROUND

M r. and Mrs. Ford watch the children at play at the Keller Kindergarten. It is obvious that the Fords were enjoying what they were doing for these children.

JOHN HARRIS

One of the most respected of all the colored citizens of the community was John Harris. Here he is shown with his two oxen and wagon near the George Washington Carver School. The field in the background is where the Carver students were taught to plant, grow, and harvest food crops. Harris maintained a small farm where he grew vegetables and canned them for winter use. He also grew sugarcane from which he made syrup to use throughout the year.

FOLLY FARMS
(FORMERLY MYRTLE GROVE)

When Mr. and Mrs. Ford came to Richmond Hill, this was the home of a wealthy lady from Pennsylvania, Mrs. Samuel Pennington Rotan. She did not sell her home or land to Mr. Ford. She had already started a clinical program treating patients in the vicinity for malaria. However, after Mr. Ford came and started an extensive drainage project to prevent malaria, built a clinic and employed several nurses and doctors to treat malaria on a large scale, Mrs. Rotan withdrew her efforts in that direction. She was a friend of the Fords and visited them when they were down here as shown by the Ford's guest book. Mrs. Rotan sold her property at Richmond Hill and bought a place in Savannah during World War II when getting gasoline was a problem. Today it is the home of Mr. and Mrs. Walter Meeks. Mr. Meeks is retired and so is his wife, Frances. Mrs. Meeks was a much loved principal of the Richmond Hill Primary School when she retired.

Myrtle Grove has an interesting history. It was part of Whitehall Plantation which was owned by Richard Arnold. Arnold owned thousands of acres in the vicinity including Cherry Hill and several other plantations in the mid eighteen hundreds. He was a very successful rice planter. It has been reported that in one year he produced one million pounds of rice. Reportedly, Arnold built this lovely home as a wedding gift to his daughter. Some readers wonder why Whitehall and Myrtle Grove were not burned by Sherman's troops during the Civil War. Both were in the vicinity of Ft. McAllister and when the troops were on their way to the fort they did not wish to reveal their presence by smoke from houses being burned.

Some readers may be interested in knowing that some of the scenes from the movie "Glory" were filmed in and around this beautiful house.

HARDWICKE

This site on the Great Ogeechee, 14 miles from the Atlantic, was selected in 1755 by Governor John Reynolds for the capital of Georgia. He named it for his kinsman, Lord High Chancellor of England, Philip Yorke Hardwicke. Reynolds said: "Hardwicke has a charming situation, the winding of the river making it a peninsula and it is the only fit place for the capital." In 1761, Sir James Wright, the Province Governor, determined against the removal of the capital from Savannah. Hardwicke then became little more than a trading village and it is now listed among "the dead towns of Georgia."

GEORGIA SOCIETY, DAUGHTERS OF THE AMERICAN COLONISTS - 1968

HARDWICKE

Today the area of Hardwicke is almost completely covered with houses. This marker, erected many years ago, beside the highway informs the visitor of the history of Hardwicke. At one time it was a very popular spot along the great Ogeechee River as evidenced by its being selected as the capital of Georgia. A plat of lots and names of lot owners is on record at the Georgia Historical Society in Savannah.

FORT MCALLISTER

When Mr. Ford bought the property on which the fort stood, the fort had deteriorated to such an extent that it was impossible to make out the details of how it had been built originally. Mr. Ford became interested in the fort and wanted it restored to its original state. He had someone do a considerable amount of research including trips to Washington to find out exactly how it was originally. He then had it restored. The fort was an earthen fort on the Ogeechee River developed at the beginning of the Civil War to provide protection for the entrance to Savannah. The Ogeechee River provided access to Savannah, only about twelve miles away. Also a short distance up the river from the fort, the Atlantic and Gulf Railroad crossed the river and it was an important supply route for the Confederates. The earthen fort was less costly than brick and could be constructed quicker. Any damage done by attacking shells could be repaired by filling with more earth using shovels and wheelbarrows. The fort was eventually taken by land action from the rear by Union forces and was destroyed. All this history seemed to interest Mr. Ford and, no doubt, influenced him to restore the fort. After the deaths of Mr. and Mrs. Ford, the fort became the property of International Paper Company. They deeded the property to the state of Georgia. It is now a state park under the Department of Natural Resources. The fort has been re-restored by the state and now is open to the public. A small museum has also been established.

JONES HOUSE

This was one of the houses in the "Bottom" Village and was built for Mr. Alva Jones who was the building architect for the plantation. Later it was the residence of Mr. Albert DeLorge who was assistant to Mr. Jones. Albert was married to Ernestine Burch, one of the daughters of William Burch who, at one time, was in charge of the sawmill. Odell Wise also assisted Mr. Jones. Odell had been through the high school at Richmond Hill and took mechanical drawing at the Industrial Arts and Trade School. He is very talented in drafting and was employed by the plantation to assist Mr. Jones.

MITCHUM HOUSE

This house was built for Mr. and Mrs. Dewey Mitchum. The Mitchums had previously lived in another house on the plantation and had boarded some of the school teachers before the teacherage was built. Mr. Mitchum was one of the early employees having come to work for the plantation in 1929. He was a labor foreman and worked as many as seventy-five in his crew at one time. They did all sorts of work, from cleaning the brick to build the Ford residence to digging drainage ditches for the housing projects. Mr. Mitchum was also one of the school trustees. The trustees worked with the Board of Education and the plantation and among other things did liaison work between the two. Mrs. Mitchum was active in the Parent Teachers Association (P.T.A.) and several other organizations. She, with some other P.T.A. members, was sent by Mr. Ford to Savannah to buy the dishes for the school lunchroom. Of course, Mr.and Mrs. Ford paid for them. They were told to buy nice dishes and in sufficient quantity to serve full meals in courses.

Mr. and Mrs. Mitchum had two children, a son, Dale, and a daughter, Carolyn, both of whom attended the Ford supported Richmond Hill School. Dale and his wife, Jacquelyn, now live in Richmond Hill.

UKKELBERG HOUSE

This house was first occupied by Mr. and Mrs. Carl Ramsey. Carl ran the commissary and his wife, Ruth, worked in the plantation office. Later it was occupied by Mr. and Mrs. Rudolph Parker. His wife, Dora, was one of the daughters of Mr. Jack Gregory, superintendent of the plantation. Rudolph was a timekeeper for the plantation and Dora was responsible for getting the Sunday program for the Martha-Mary Chapel put together and seeing that the program was printed and available at the chapel on Sunday. The next occupant was Mr. and Mrs. Harry G. Ukkelberg. Mr. Ukkelberg was director of the research laboratory and in charge of the general farming operations and including the experimental plantings of various crops. Mrs. Ukkelberg, Blanche, was a part time nurse at the Ford clinic. The house came to be known as the Ukkelberg house. This photo was taken after the passing of Mr. and Mrs. Ford as evidenced by the red trim. Neither Mr. or Mrs. Ford cared for red. All the Ford buildings at Richmond Hill were painted white and none were trimmed in red during their lifetime.

Today, the house is the property of George A. Waters, Attorney at Law, and he uses it as his office. It has been repainted and is in excellent condition.

OFFICE MANAGER'S HOUSE

The name does not fit the case in all circumstances. This house was originally built for another one of the superintendent's daughters Nancy and her husband Stuart Carpenter who at that time was manager of he commissary. It was later occupied by Mr.and Mrs. Ben Brewton and family. Mr. Brewton at that time was manager of the plantation office. The office manager before him was Robbie Thomson but he lived in Savannah. Anyway, the house became known as the office manager's house. Today it is owned and occupied by Mr. and Mrs. Ray Arnsdorf. Mrs. Arnsdorf was formerly Mary Helen Smith and was one of the students who received such excellent training in home economics at the Ford Community House.

BURCH HOUSE

This house was built for Mr. William Burch who, at that time, was in charge of the sawmill. Although this house was built more than fifty years ago, it has not been significantly altered except for the color of the paint. Mr. and Mrs. Burch had seven children all of whom attended the Richmond Hill School and thereby received the excellent training made possible by Mr. Ford's generosity. They were: Ernestine, Martha, Doris, William, Frances, Betty, and Carol.

In the mid-forties Mr. Burch took a job in North Carolina and moved his family there. Soon thereafter the McAllister family moved into the house. They had five children, all of whom attended the Richmond Hill School. The children were: Earl, Betty Lou, Helen, Tommy, and Leo.

An interesting note is that neither Mr. or Mrs. McAllister worked for the plantation. Both were depot agents. Mr. McAllister was depot agent for the Atlantic Coastline Railroad in Richmond Hill and Mrs McAllister was employed as railroad agent a few miles south of Richmond Hill. In helping people, Mr. Ford made no distinction between employees and non-employees. He helped all.

HOBBS HOUSE

This house was built for Mrs. Vera Hobbs. She did not work for the plantation but was depot agent for the Seaboard Railroad that ran through Richmond Hill. However she did have a son, Junior, who worked at the gas department for the plantation. Her daughter, Edith, worked for the post office. This clearly shows that Mr. Ford wanted to help others too not just those who worked for him on the plantation. His generosity in helping others was almost beyond belief.

An historical note concerning the post office and the railroad may be of interest to the younger readers. At that time much of the mail going out of the local area was carried by train. The out going mail was placed in a canvas bag that had a loop rope on top and bottom. This was carried to the railroad and hung on the rack adjacent to the railroad track. The passenger train had a mail car and in this mail car there was a metal arm that swung out and caught the mail bag and pulled it into the mail car and the mail was on its way. The train might be traveling sixty miles per hour but the metal arm grabbed the mail with no problem. In the case of Richmond Hill, a very fast traveling passenger train came through at 11 a.m. on the Coastline Railroad and got the mail. One of Edith Hobbs' jobs was to get the bag of mail to the railroad and place it on the rack for the train to pick it up at 11 a.m.

CARPENTER HOUSE

This house was built for Mr. and Mrs. Dick Carpenter. Dick worked in the Ford cabinet shop and his wife, Pearl, was in charge of the school lunchrooms at Richmond Hill and the Carver School. This is a fairly recent photo of the house, but it has not been altered except for the color of the paint. When Mr. Ford had the houses built for employees, they were all painted white – no exceptions. The framing around the window screens were usually painted black. All the houses had hardwood floors which were kept varnished and refinished as needed.

The Carpenters had four children who went through the Ford supported schools. They are: Harry, Evelyn, Bobby, and Bertie. Bobby and Bertie are both married and live in Richmond Hill. Bobby was postmaster at Richmond Hill for many years prior to his retirement.

SCHOOL PRINCIPAL'S HOUSE

This house was built by Mr. Ford for the school principal. It was diagonally across the street from the school and therefore very convenient. Occupancy changed with a change in principal. Today it is the home of Mrs. Wilbur Yawn. Mr. Yawn passed in 1997. He had attended the Richmond Hill School. Mrs. Yawn is the granddaughter of Mrs. Vera Hobbs whose house is shown elsewhere as the Hobbs house.

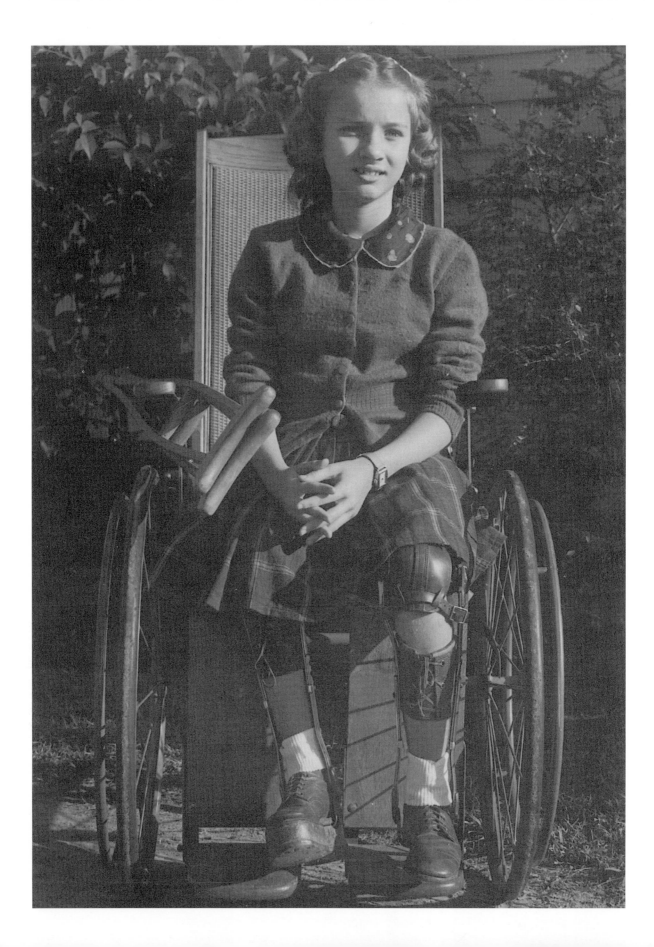

MARY LOU MARTIN
AND THE MARTIN HOUSE

Mary Lou is the daughter of Aimar and Rose Martin of Richmond Hill. Mr. Martin was bookkeeper for the Ford Plantation. He passed away in 1978. Mrs. Martin still lives in Richmond Hill. Mary Lou is the victim of polio. This photo was taken about 1943.

Mr. Ford, being aware of her handicap, sent her up to Dearborn to the Ford Hospital for a year of free treatment. When she returned to Richmond Hill, he built her family a home within a block of the school so she could be near the school. Today, the house is the home of Mr. and Mrs. Leon Judy. Mrs. Judy worked in the plantation office and later worked for International Paper Company who purchased the plantation after the death of Mr. and Mrs. Ford. The house has been enlarged over the years.

Mr. Ford gave her the wheelchair she is sitting in. Through the courtesy of the Martin family, the chair is now at the Richmond Hill Historical Society Museum.

Mary Lou is one of the most admirable persons I have ever known. Despite her handicap she completed high school and went on to college and obtained a degree in education and taught school. She is a very talented lady and, among other things, is an accomplished musician. She plays the piano and sings with a beautiful voice. In addition, she is married and has four children. With her handicap, her accomplishments seem impossible but they are real. In addition to all this, she always has a smile and has a very pleasant personality. I greatly admire her and her accomplishments.

THE LONG HOUSE

This house was built for Leslie and Lucy Long (authors of this book). He worked in the Ford Research Laboratory and she was mathematics and science teacher in the Richmond Hill High School. During the summers she worked in the research laboratory. She worked as payroll clerk in the plantation office from late 1949 until the plantation office closed after the death or Mr. and Mrs. Ford. This house, like most of the others, had a building in back for an automobile, a laundry room, and a place for firewood storage. In addition, it had a garden area of about one-half acre.

THE BELL HOUSE

This house was built for Mr. and Mrs. Joseph Columbus Bell. He was employed by the Ford Plantation and his wife, Carrie, was Bryan County Home Demonstration Agent. Their oldest son, Fulton, was in charge of the Industrial Arts and Trade School. Their next son, John, was in charge of the Cabinet Shop and was responsible for the fine furniture they made. A younger son, Joe C., attended the Richmond Hill School. Today, the Bell house is the home of Mr. and Mrs. David Butler. Very recently, the Butlers sold their property and the house was moved to the Keller community. A chain grocery is to be built on the property.

"THE WOODS RIDERS"

These men, left to right are: Enoch Dukes, Tom Darieng, Rad Davis, and "Buck" Ellis. These men were the ones who rode the woods, primarily at night, to prevent illegal hunting. Mr. Ford insisted on protecting the wildfire on the plantation. There were lots of deer on the plantation and there were some problems with people hunting deer with lights at night, so called "fire hunting". They would shine a bright light on the deer and their eyes would reflect the light and they would shoot them. It was the responsibility of these men to prevent this practice. They were deputized by the county and had authority to arrest the violators.

Once a field of soybeans was being eaten by deer. Mr. Ford was advised of this and his answer was "plant enough for the deer too".

Another responsibility of the "woods riders" was to confiscate illegal moonshine stills of which I have first hand information. I was working in the research laboratory and we wanted to determine the yield of alcohol from various crops such as sweet potatoes. This involved fermentation and distillation. We took one of the moonshine stills that had been confiscated and set it up outside in back of the laboratory to make the distillations. We had it fixed up very nice including bricking in the still. We had only made a few distillations when one night the still disappeared. Apparently, one of the moonshiners wanted his still back. There were night watchman around but somehow they were evaded.

HENRY FORD
CIRCA 1940

A rare photo of Mr. Ford relaxing on the front steps of his residence at Richmond Hill.

A Sad Day

This was one of the saddest days that Richmond Hill ever experienced when the moving van came to take away the Ford's belongings from their residence. The people of Richmond Hill loved the Fords and appreciated so very much what they had done for them. There was a closeness there beyond description. This was particularly true for the Fords employees. The Fords had been coming to Richmond Hill for nearly twenty-five years and just to think about it was all ending was very sad. Their coming each year was looked forward to with joyful anticipation. They had always come and gone but now reality was expressing itself that they would not be back. Two other extremely sad days were when Mr. Ford died on April 7, 1947, and Mrs. Ford on Sept. 29, 1950, but somehow this seemed to be the saddest day of all when the residence was emptied and they would be there no more.

EPILOGUE

Mr. Ford passed away April 7, 1947, soon after he returned to Dearborn from Richmond Hill. Mrs. Ford passed away September 29, 1950. Mr. Ford had told employees that he had arranged for the plantation to continue to operate after his and Mrs. Ford's death. Despite his efforts and plans, it did not turn out that way. In November of 1951, the plantation property, encompassing about 80,000 acres or 125 square miles, was sold to International Paper Company. According to records in the Bryan County Courthouse, the purchase price was about five and one-half million dollars. International Paper Company was primarily interested in the timber and soon sold off most of the buildings, including the numerous homes Mr. Ford had built for the employees. Most of the houses were bought by the occupants who had worked for the plantation. The Martha-Mary Chapel was purchased by the Catholic Church and is now St. Anne's Catholic Church. The Community House changed hands several times and is presently Stewart Brothers Funeral Services. A chapel has been built in connection with it and is named the Ford Chapel. An oil painting of Mr. Ford is inside.

International Paper Company sold the Ford residence together with 1800 acres separately. It changed ownership several times over the years. At one time, the residence was operated as a restaurant. Later, the restaurant was discontinued and the building deteriorated to an unsightly condition. Still later, it became the property of Ghaith Pharaon, a Saudi Arabian businessman. He repaired and remodeled the residence, powerhouse, and grounds. This included the installation of a swimming pool between the residence and the river, and building a golf course. Pharaon was later indicted for bank fraud in the Bank of Credit and Commerce International (BCCI) scandal and left the country. In May of 1998, a group of developers from Hilton Head Island, South Carolina, purchased the old Ford residence and 1620 acres for a reported price of 30 million dollars. They purchased an additional 63 acres for five million dollars. According to newspaper reports, they plan to develop upscale recreational homes with yacht docking facilities, fishing, golfing, hunting, and other recreational facilities. The Ford residence is to be used as a clubhouse for the homeowners. It has been reported that a choice waterfront lot and house will cost about one million dollars. There is physical evidence that the project is already underway.

Bryan County was cut in two parts in 1940 when the federal government purchased land for Fort Stewart, leaving a north part and a south part. Today, the total county population is approximately 23,000, about 60 percent of which is in south Bryan. Within the city limits of Richmond Hill, there are approximately 6000 and about 7500 in the unincorporated area. Richmond Hill is one of the fastest growing areas in Georgia. It has, to a large extent, become a "bedroom" of Savannah. It is a very desirable place to live due, in part, to the excellent schools.

They rank near the top in the state. A great deal of the credit should go to Mr. Ford who provided outstanding facilities and financial assistance to the school in the thirties and forties. People of the Richmond Hill area have come to expect the best in schools. Today, Richmond Hill has four schools, a primary, elementary, middle, and high school, with a fifth in the planning stage.

INDEX

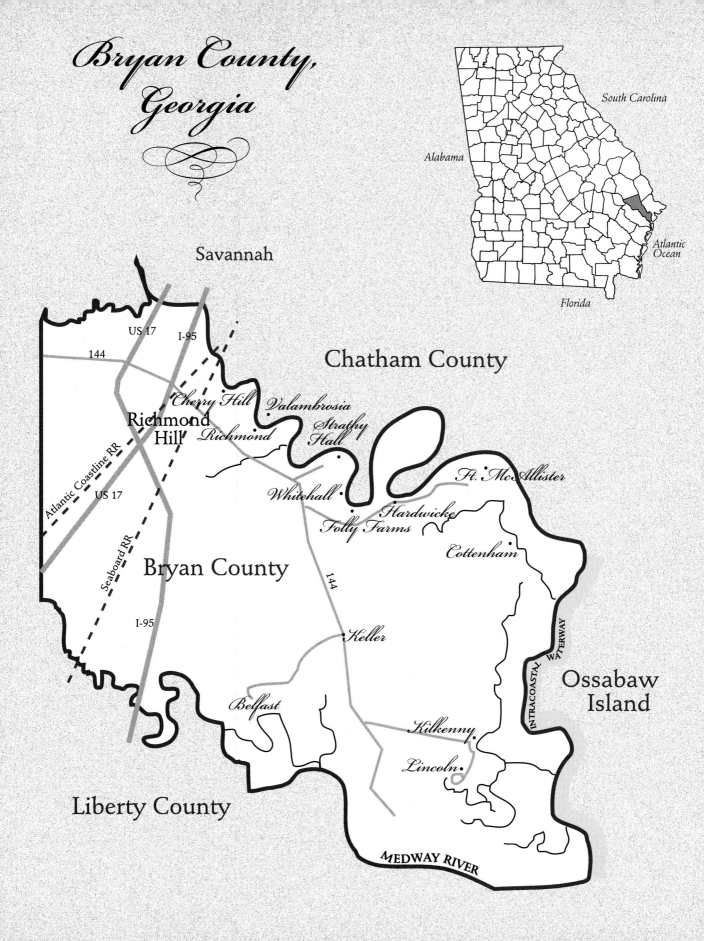

Bryan County, Georgia

South Carolina

Alabama

Atlantic Ocean

Florida

Savannah

US 17   I-95

144

Chatham County

Cherry Hill

Valambrosia

Richmond Hill

Richmond

Straffy Hall

Ft. McAllister

Whitehall

Hardwicke

Folly Farms

Atlantic Coastline RR

US 17

Bryan County

Cottenham

Seaboard RR

144

I-95

Keller

Ossabaw Island

Belfast

Kilkenny

INTRACOASTAL WATERWAY

Lincoln

Liberty County

MEDWAY RIVER